Cambridge Eler

Elements in Business Str
edited by
J.-C. Spender
Rutgers Business School

TOOLS FOR STRATEGY

A Starter Kit for Academics and Practitioners

Henri Hakala
Lappeenranta University of Technology

Tero Vuorinen
HAUS Finnish Institute of Public Management

CAMBRIDGE
UNIVERSITY PRESS

University Printing House, Cambridge CB2 8BS, United Kingdom

One Liberty Plaza, 20th Floor, New York, NY 10006, USA

477 Williamstown Road, Port Melbourne, VIC 3207, Australia

314–321, 3rd Floor, Plot 3, Splendor Forum, Jasola District Centre,
New Delhi – 110025, India

79 Anson Road, #06–04/06, Singapore 079906

Cambridge University Press is part of the University of Cambridge.

It furthers the University's mission by disseminating knowledge in the pursuit of
education, learning, and research at the highest international levels of excellence.

www.cambridge.org
Information on this title: www.cambridge.org/9781108793193
DOI: 10.1017/9781108883757

First published 2020

A catalogue record for this publication is available from the British Library.

ISBN 978-1-108-79319-3 Paperback
ISSN 2515-0693 (online)
ISSN 2515-0685 (print)

Tools for Strategy

A Starter Kit for Academics and Practitioners

Elements in Business Strategy

DOI: 10.1017/9781108883757
First published online: August 2020

Henri Hakala
Lappeenranta University of Technology

Tero Vuorinen
HAUS Finnish Institute of Public Management

Author for correspondence: Henri Hakala, henri.hakala@lut.fi

Abstract: This Element discusses the concept and applications of strategy tools. Strategy tools are frameworks, techniques, and methods that help individuals and organizations to create their strategies. After a brief overview of different ideas on strategy and strategic thinking, we move on to define and discuss what strategy tools are and elaborate on the promise and perils of using them to implement strategic management. We review the most commonly used, classic tools and techniques but also less well-known tools of the strategy trade, as proposed by scholars writing in the leading strategy journals. We conclude by offering suggestions on how to improve strategic design and the effectiveness of the resultant strategy through the selective use of the most appropriate tools. Overall, this Element provides a quick overview of the tools that are available to those tasked with creating organizational strategies and making strategic decisions.

Keywords: strategy, strategy tools, decision-making, rational analysis, business & entrepreneurship

ISBNs: 9781108793193 (PB), 9781108883757 (OC)
ISSNs: 2515-0693 (online), 2515-0685 (print)

Contents

1 Introduction

Anyone intent on doing a job properly needs to know what tools of the trade are available. Surprisingly, for those whose job is strategy – whether practitioners, academics, or students – those tools of the trade are not easily found in one place, and strategists will most likely have to work through fragmented knowledge on strategy tools located in a number of places. The purpose of this Element is to introduce the concept of strategy tools and to outline the variety of tools available to strategists today. The Element should prove a useful starter kit for anyone requiring a brief overview of the tools that are available to those tasked with creating organizational strategies. *Strategy tools are frameworks, techniques, and methods that help individuals and organizations to create their strategies* – in other words, to determine what is, will, or should be done to address issues central to the success of the organization, usually beyond the short and medium term. Recently, a group of prominent scholars in the field of strategy called for more research on strategy tools because such tools can both enable and constrain strategy making (Burgelman et al., 2018). Therefore, this Element aims to provide a useful and accessible introduction to the topic of strategy tools for academics interested in strategy and in response to that call.

For practitioners, strategy tools should help create and deliver better strategies; however, as there is no strategy that will always be right, there cannot be a tool guaranteed to work every time. Strategists should therefore understand the workings of more than one tool, and the core point of reading this Element is to familiarize yourself with a number of different tools and thereby expand your theories in use. Beyond describing some of the most useful strategy tools, we hope to give strategists the confidence to select and develop versions and combinations of tools that work to deliver their own needs. There is no toolkit that would work for all purposes, and the most appropriate tools are those that will help to address the problems and knowledge gaps pertaining to each current situation. One should use tools creatively and often and learn more by using them.

We first briefly introduce the concept of strategic management because its focus – organizational strategy – could be perceived as a management tool in itself (Section 2). Strategy is a tool in the sense that it is there to help organizations negotiate, determine, and achieve their objectives or performance targets. After a brief overview of different ideas on what constitutes both strategy and strategic thinking, we move on to define and discuss what strategy tools are (Section 3) before we elaborate on the promise and the perils of using them to implement strategic management (Section 4).

Section 5 introduces some of the best-known strategy tools. These are tools that we suggest any manager, strategist, or student of strategy should at least be able to describe the key tenets of. We then move on to review some of the less well-known tools and techniques that we believe to be interesting and which constitute potentially useful options in the strategist's toolbox (Section 6). The tools we present are the result of reviewing the publications of the leading strategy and general management journals spanning the past twenty-five years to find articles introducing new strategy tools. While the space here is limited, we provide citations to the original works that will allow the reader to discover more about those tools, which then makes it possible for interested readers to search the Internet to access additional information. We do not claim to have found all the tools available, and we are certainly aware that many strategy tools have not even featured in academic journals, because many are only comprehensively explained in books or remain the proprietary secrets of strategy professionals or consultants. In Sections 7–8, we also outline some conceptual areas that do not appear to be served by strategy tools. Finally, this book concludes with our thoughts on how strategy work could be improved with the tools we review and others still unknown to us, and we also offer tips on how to build your own strategist's toolbox.

2 Strategy As a Tool for Strategic Management?

Strategy itself is a tool for strategic management, but no one seems able to agree on what kind of tool. Textbooks conventionally describe strategic management as an activity that supports the long-term success of an organization. Whereas operational management focuses on today, tomorrow, and next week, strategic management is about the coming months, years, or decades. Strategy has been described as a recipe for success, as a formula for a profitable company, and as a theory of business operations. However it is labelled, the strategy of the firm is one of the central concepts in management research and there are numerous different definitions and ways of thinking about such a strategy. One textbook definition of a business strategy is that it 'defines and communicates what an entity creates, by whom, how, for whom and why it is valuable' (Huff et al., 2009, p. 21) but there are many more ideas and definitions. Most definitions seem to suggest that strategy is a result of a series of procedures implemented to help an organization achieve success in the future: it is a conscious, purposeful effort to choose a direction for the organization in an ever-changing environment. A good strategy gives an organization a sense of direction and meaning, creating an organizational identity and thus helping employees act in a coherent manner; or, as Spender (2014) puts it, strategy brings together the identity, intention, and situation in reasoned action.

To cement this coherent, purposeful, and reasoned behaviour of organizational members, employees in a work community have 'a right' to be led, and supervisors have 'a duty' to lead, whether they want to or not. Without any leadership from a supervisor, or at least strong arrangements that allow for self-organizing, employees cannot be successful at work and there is likely to be frustration and uncertainty in the work community. Following this logic, an organization has an obligation to create a strategy to enable supervisors and other members of management to perform their leadership tasks. The organization's employees should be aware of their roles and tasks and of their part in the larger role and ambitions of the organization. This kind of knowledge is created through strategy; however, organizations are not generally under any legal obligation to devise or publish a strategy,[1] and organizations craft strategies because they consider them useful ways to improve the performance and success of the organization. While the performance of an organization can also be influenced by many other factors beyond the control of its management, the concept of strategy has become one of the major tools in itself. Strategy has come to be viewed as a tool that helps to grasp the things that affect organizational direction and performance as well as a tool that managers *believe* that they can use to influence the performance of the organization they are managing.

Performance is a key term for strategy. In business, performance usually refers to financial success and shareholders receiving dividends on their investment, but organizational performance can also be perceived in many other ways. Researchers generally agree that organizational performance is a multidimensional construct and recognize that different organizational strategies and activities may have different effects on the dimensions of organizational performance. Performance may first be divided into operational and organizational performance measures, and then organizational performance may be further divided into dimensions of accounting returns, stock market returns, and growth (Combs et al., 2005). The measures assigned to these dimensions tend to be further classified into objective and subjective measures. The objective indicators include profit in comparison to turnover, assets, or investment, which in turn might either be compared with that of competitors within the industry or be treated as absolute numbers. Growth is another common measure

---

[1] Generally in the sense that, for example, UK-incorporated companies must include a strategic report in their annual report. The strategic report reviews the company's business and describes the risks and uncertainties facing the company. Small companies are exempt from this requirement.

and can encompass growth in profits, sales, market share, or number of employees, whereas the most common stock market success measures are stock returns and market-to-book-value ratios (Combs et al., 2005). Subjective measures can also take many forms but can be characterized by their aim to assess performance in light of the prevailing situation. For example, a firm may be viewed objectively as making losses, but its performance could be deemed successful if those losses have reduced year on year. Alternatively, if the economy is sluggish and profit and growth levels marginal, a firm's performance might be compared to that of its competitors and, even in the absence of growth per se, could be presented as doing well in the circumstances. Subjectively, performance might also be assessed to be adequate or successful if a particular project has progressed according to plan or if the firm has demonstrated an ability to learn how to deal with certain difficult issues, so that its staff perceive it to be doing something well. For a public-sector or non-profit organization, a strategy might, for example, aim to reduce the use of unhealthy substances by citizens, or protect the rainforests, or boost entrepreneurship in a region or nationally. In that case, success cannot be measured in monetary terms but will be assessed on the progress towards other goals. Nevertheless, we would argue that each of the schools of thought in the realm of strategy essentially appear to share a common interest in understanding, explaining, or predicting organizational performance. Accordingly, the strategic tools capable of delivering the required performance will differ depending on the type of performance the organization aspires to.

Strategies can and should be devised at different levels of abstraction. A corporate-level strategy should address the field of business the organization engages in. In contrast, a function-level strategy will be designed to maximize resource productivity within that specific function. In between those two, business level strategies are designed to address the question of effectively competing in each of the chosen product–market segments. The strategy tools appropriate for different layers of strategy may differ, or the same tools may be used differently to achieve the required level of abstraction. Porter (1980/2008) suggested that the performance of firms is dependent on the choice of industry and that different industries attract different levels of performance. On the other hand, the resource-based school of thought on strategy suggests that the performance of an organization has far more to do with the resources it has to deploy rather than the choice of industry. The moderate position between the extremes might be that the better an organization understands its own position, in terms of the environment it operates in, its competitors, the interest groups that affect it, and its own capabilities, the better choices that organization is able to make and the more effectively it will conduct actions flowing from its choices. However, in the field of strategy there are many different ways of being right and many different methods of reaching an equally acceptable result. Strategy literature offers many different schools of thought (see e.g. Minzberg et al., 2005) that define strategy in different ways and have their own specific interests. Some writers emphasize the importance of planning, while others focus on learning and experience-based strategy, and others still talk about innovation and experimentation. The truth is that one can never be completely certain of the effectiveness and effects of strategic management. When the economy is booming, people like to talk about how success clearly resulted from selecting the right strategy, whereas during a slump they place the blame on bad luck and unfavourable conditions. We like to think of strategy as something more than just a plan. While planning is a useful exercise if you know where you are going, the goal is more than often quite unclear, and strategy becomes more about coping with uncertainty than planning.

Using strategy to cope with uncertainty. Historically, people's relationship with strategy has changed. The most recent, large-scale changes have been, for example, a closer connection between the planning and implementation stages of strategy, the desire to involve employees in making strategy, and a shift away from analysing and adapting to the environment to developing and exploiting competences in innovative ways. In many cases, rather than speaking of strategic management, it would be more appropriate to speak of holistic and participation-focused *strategic thinking* extending throughout the organization. Arguably, with the increased popularity of the strategy concept has also come a shift down from group-level strategies to more delimited, business-unit strategies. At the same time, organizations have learned to live with the fact that they cannot plan as meticulously as they once did. As we live in a world where nothing is certain, organizations must cope with constant uncertainty. As Minzberg and Waters (1985) argued, the strategy that organizations aim for is quite often something significantly different from the strategy they get. Indeed, we would align ourselves with the thought that strategy is better understood as a constant striving for competitive advantage rather than the long-term planning and implementation of fixed plans; that is, strategy is partially deliberate direction and actions but with twists and turns along the way that serve to advance it. As a result, strategy constantly mutates into something different.

In practice, strategic management is never a coherent process. If we look at what people who are involved with strategy making do, it is clear that they are implementing hundreds or thousands of processes, both in sequence and in parallel. All strategy-making projects will be liable to occasionally grinding to a standstill owing to the likes of time pressures, meetings, work trips, and sick leave. For that reason, we should not be alarmed if strategic management does not manifest itself as a clear and simple process. We must remember that the work of a manager is never just one continuous process, regardless of whether we are talking about strategy or operations. While the world is not clear or well organized, it is important to try to organize and analyse even the difficult and ambiguous aspects, to discuss them, and constantly seek to develop them. Strategic thinking is a professional skill that can be acquired and internalized just like delivering on quality standards, projecting and upholding accurate delivery times, or maintaining excellent customer service levels. Therefore, strategic thinking is a *competence*, not some form of semi-mystical rain dance performed once a year.

Within strategic management literature, many scholars distinguish between the strategy content and strategy process perspectives. The content perspective argues that competitive advantage results from the content of strategies that relate to competitors, customers, or uniquely valuable resource combinations or positions in the markets. As such, the content perspective attempts to explain *what strategy should be about*. In turn, the process perspective argues that competitive advantage results from processes such as analysis and planning, learning and development, or entrepreneurial behaviours or attempts to explain *how firms should act*, how strategies are implemented, or how organizations go about devising their strategies. A third, more recent addition to the main research perspectives is the strategy-as-practice (SAP) approach. The SAP stream of research focuses on practitioners (i.e. the people involved in strategy); practices (e.g. the tools, norms, traditions, concepts, shared routines, and reflection procedures); and praxis (i.e. the activities involved in strategy making) (e.g. Jarzabkowski, 2005; Whittington, 2006), which has been summarized by Golsorkhi and colleagues as, '[SAP] focuses on the micro-level social activities, processes and practices that characterize organizational strategy and strategizing' (Golsorkhi et al., 2010, p. 1). While SAP may be less interested in the formal strategy documents and more in what is actually done when constructing and implementing strategy (Golsorkhi et al., 2010), it also shares an interest in strategy tools. Scholars investigating the SAP approach have looked at strategy tools as something that people use in their strategic praxis. Strategy tools can be viewed as one manifestation of strategy theory in use, and SAP researchers have focused their attention on the various manifestations of strategy tools, which include their role as boundary objects (Spee and Jarzabkowski, 2009), as technologies of rationality (Jarzabkowski and Kaplan, 2015), and as vehicles of visualization (Paroutis et al., 2015). However, not everyone is exercised by these distinctions between different schools of thought. Practising managers integrate different views and perceive strategy as a holistic combination of processes, content, and practices. Individuals have very different ideas about strategy, and because what is strategically important varies across different environments, industries, or firms, the idea of what constitutes a good strategy is not a simple one.

To summarize this section, strategy is a relatively broadly (and sometimes even badly) defined tool in itself that can be used to pursue performance and to cope with the uncertainty of not knowing what is going to happen. Performance is multidimensional and depends on the purpose of the organization. Therefore, strategies may be devised on different levels of abstraction and may take different forms. Strategy could tell us what we do, how we do it, and when we do it, but also why we do it. However, while strategy itself can be a tool to facilitate achieving the objectives of the organization, the term *strategy tool* more commonly denotes more detailed frameworks, processes, or techniques designed to help individuals craft appropriate strategies.

3 What Are Strategy Tools and Techniques?

Tools, in general, are devices that are used to carry out a particular function. Logically, then, strategy tools are something that can be used to craft or construct strategies. They can take many shapes and forms, but as a group they are abstract frameworks, processes, or techniques that aim to help individuals construct better strategies for themselves, their teams, their business units, their firm, or an organization of any kind. There is no specific stream of literature dedicated solely to strategy tools, and they have been developed across different disciplines and from very different theoretical starting points. Nevertheless, it seems reasonable to expect that, whatever the school of thought, the aim of a strategy tool is to assist in constructing strategies that improve organizational performance in some way or another.

Bearing in mind the multiple schools of thought on what constitutes a strategy, it is also challenging to determine exactly what constitutes a strategy tool. Some might consider budgeting, market research, or customer satisfaction surveys, or the simple use of spreadsheets or cost accounting methods to be strategic tools. Customer satisfaction measurement should be standard practice for any larger firm these days, yet many smaller ones may still ignore any formal assessment of their customer satisfaction. However, rather than a tool for strategy making per se, a certain level of customer satisfaction is often set as a target, similar to profitability, growth, or turnover. Certainly, many strategy tools encompass measures of customer satisfaction or, more broadly, listening to customers or a customer value perspective, yet it is difficult to see that the customer satisfaction survey itself should be described as a strategy tool.

It is more likely to be assessed as one input to be considered or something that measures how well an organization achieves its customer satisfaction objectives.

Some scholars might perceive mission and vision statements as tools. However, it is questionable whether the various statements of the mission, vision, or values of an organization constitute a strategy-making tool in any strict sense. Clearly, the idea of stating something is a mission, objective, or corporate value, and particularly the process of formulating such statements, may serve to set the parameters of what the firm strategy should look like – just as any number of things said out loud, written down as strategy, and made known by the organization's staff or customers will direct people's thoughts and actions and have properties that guide thinking and interactions in management teams (Spee and Jarzabkowski, 2009). Accordingly, we see various mission and vision statements as *outcomes* of the use of strategy tools. Similarly, calculating different break-even points or return on investment and various types of cash flow analysis are important aspects of strategic decision-making and provide simplified information that could support making strategic judgements. Whether they constitute a strategic tool as such is a trickier question. In a way, a break-even point calculation represents a simple form of scenario analysis, allowing the strategist to manipulate price, demand, and costs to establish the point at which the business or product becomes profitable. Nevertheless, what we perceive here as strategy tools generally have a more defined processual character, and hence act more like technologies of rationality (Jarzabkowski and Kaplan, 2015) or as vehicles of visualization (Paroutis et al., 2015).

While there is no comprehensive answer to the question of where we could draw the line between strategy or some other generic management tool, many things do, in some way, support the decision-making process, efficiency, profitability, quality control, marketing, or some other dimensions of the company's field of business. The line between a strategy tool and a management tool is also blurred; for example, Bain & Company describe *strategic planning* as the most frequently used management tool.[2] Other concepts listed in the consultancy's top-ten list of management tools include customer relationship management (CRM), benchmarking, advanced analytics, supply chain management,

---

[2] In an article on Bain & Company's website, the company suggests that 'Strategic Planning is a comprehensive process for determining what a business should become and how it can best achieve that goal. It appraises the full potential of a business and explicitly links the business's objectives to the actions and resources required to achieve them. Strategic Planning offers a systematic process to ask and answer the most critical questions confronting a management team – especially large, irrevocable resource commitment decisions' (see www.bain.com/publica tions/articles/management-tools-strategic-planning.aspx; accessed 16 April 2018).

customer satisfaction, change management, total quality management (TQM), digital transformation, and mission/vision statements.

Our approach to defining what constitutes a strategy tool is somewhat broader than just strategic planning but somewhat narrower than the above-mentioned notion of management tools. We would describe strategy tools as sources of advice on and aids to strategic thinking. Strategy tools both reflect and shape the current thinking on strategy and have an important role to play when managers undertake the labour of strategy or so-called strategic praxis. Studies on the popularity of strategy tools and on their usefulness have ascribed them properties that guide thinking and interactions among top and middle management. If we consider that, in addition, business schools commonly instruct aspiring managers in the use of strategy tools, the potential impact of the tools extends far into the future, to contexts we cannot really imagine.

In sum, we have adopted the very broad perspective that strategy is some sort of idea (even if sometimes a formal plan) denoting what the company is or what it should be doing; it follows that *strategy tools are something used in the strategy process to create content for the strategic praxis.* Hence, strategy tools might also guide how the strategy process is organized and how the strategy is implemented. Some strategy tools are simple frameworks that list a number of potential issues, whereas others are highly structured processes or even artificial intelligence–powered market analysis. In all cases, strategy tools help to determine what is, will, or should be done in terms of issues perceived to be important to the success of the organization.

4 The Promise and Perils of Strategy Tools

Strategy tools usually promise improvements in performance, profitability, revenues, or innovation to anyone who is alert and smart enough to use them. A company or manager applying a strategy tool will understand the organization's current business environment, including the opportunities, threats, and trends present in the markets the organization holds an interest in. A firm applying a strategy tool might aim to maximize its revenue from current customers by designing its product and service offerings to fit with its current customers' perceptions of value. It might also be able to attract new customers by offering something better – in the sense of something more valuable – than its competitors' offerings. It might also see where the market is going and be prepared for changes in customer preferences, be able to anticipate competitor moves, and be prepared for regulatory changes as well as the threat posed by new kinds of competitor and substitutive products. It might be able to look further into the future than its competitors and possibly shape the future in a way that suits the competencies of the firm. Some tools can also help to optimize market and product portfolios and provide competitive advantages through a clever business model design. A firm using strategy tools might also learn to know itself and its resources; it might understand the extent of its capabilities and competencies and thus be equipped to avoid the pitfalls of over-optimism and unwise investments. A firm that can accurately analyse the resources, capabilities, and competencies of its competitors and customers would gain an advantage in targeting the most productive market niches, with the most effective kinds of messages, and perhaps be able to avoid resource-sapping battles with its stronger competitors. Through understanding its value chains and pertinent business logics, such a firm would understand how its operational decision-making could be refined to deliver improved earnings. In other words, firms employing strategy tools might be able to turn their disadvantages into advantages. It is important to note that, while strategic thinking is important, strategies must be turned into actions, which is another key function of any strategy tool. Strategy tools might promise a lot, but they deliver only when used wisely. Unfortunately, management can often be tempted to equate smart management with obtaining a range of strategy tools and slavishly implementing their recommendations.

It is important to acknowledge that tools cannot do the work for the strategist; realistically however, they can give structure to that strategist's work. In so doing, they can help to alleviate the stress of coping with various uncertainties, or knowledge absences,[3] and hence help make a judgement (right at the time, but time will tell).

Strategy work itself is often ill-defined. The business environment contains many uncertainties, but then if business opportunities were clear to all protagonists the opportunity would soon disappear for any party other than the original discoverer, or the firm able to market the goods or services flowing from the opportunity at the lowest cost. As competition gets tougher, the party that sees things most clearly and implements the most viable strategy wins the battle. In the midst of this struggle, many pairs of eyes will probably see better than one, and the multi-perspective approach can be vital when business opportunities exist only in certain environments and for limited periods. Accordingly, a wise organization will involve a wider selection of staff than just the top management

---

[3] Spender (2014) suggests that strategy work has three types of knowledge absences that complicate the life of the strategist: (1) ignorance of what can be known – lack of data and understanding of the goal and ways to get there; (2) incommensurability – while fragmented data is available, there is the problem of connecting the dots and the absence of understanding of how much we know; and (3) indeterminacy – whatever we decide to do in the environment, the people, firms, and other actors within it respond in ways we cannot predict, and their reactions do not remain constant over time, even if we simply repeat our actions.

team in its strategy-making process. Strategy tools can provide a vehicle for engaging a range of staff members in that strategy-making process, in so far as appropriate strategy tools can provide common frameworks and a language that can be learned by everyone in the organization.

Despite the undoubted potential of strategy tools, management should be sceptical of any tools offered to their organization. Tools generally simplify and classify a fuzzy reality, but the world is actually very complicated; so, while simplifications can help to grasp the world, they are not a true reflection of it. Quite often, when we say that things are complex, it just means that we do not understand them ourselves, and that is usually down to not knowing enough about them. Nevertheless, the epithet *Keep It Simple Stupid* is often suggested to be a good rule for making strategies actionable. While we agree that strategies should be comprehensible to whoever is supposed to action them, we prefer to view strategies as involving a web of often complex issues that should not be simplified *too much*. Anecdotally, Albert Einstein himself was reported to have suggested that everything should be made as simple as possible, but no simpler. Strategy tools help to add to our knowledge and hence reduce the complexity in our minds.

In addition to being comprehensible, strategies should also be capable of adaptation to suit changing circumstances. Of course, if a firm's strategic decisions involved large investments in physical resources, the strategy cannot easily be reversed without major ramifications, but that is not the point here. The traditional approach based on rational planning and the assumption that a business will be dealing with a smart customer whose will can be anticipated may simply no longer be apposite in a world where there is an abundance of everything. Once people have secured a roof over their heads, enough food, and fulfilled some other basic needs, some are prone to make choices the majority of people would find baffling, such as spending a mint on a useless two-seater sports car that cannot even be driven on public roads or thousands on 'diamonds' in an online game. What this implies for the use of strategy tools, when their assumption is to rationalize and estimate the customer behaviour based on historical patterns, is that they should be taken with a good pinch of salt. The outcomes may reflect past experiences more accurately than they safeguard the organization against future shocks.

Nevertheless, not everything changes all the time. There are markets in which competition is not so fierce, and people will not constantly change their learned behaviours. In many cases, it may still be wise to use several tools and methods and see if the conclusions from the application of the various data align, even if not seamlessly. One should not take strategy tools too seriously or slavishly implement the outcomes the tools suggest; tools do not build a house, humans do, and, when implementing strategy, conducting a reality check is always worthwhile. There is inevitably a simple 'meme' to do that too: the three questions introduced by Day (2007) – 'Is it real?', 'Can we win?', and 'Is it worth doing?' – are worth asking before taking almost any strategic decision.

It would be very unusual for a strategist to start constructing a strategy from the base position of having no idea of where the problem lies or of what should be analysed. The choice of the strategy tool is, in this respect, a vehicle for discerning what is important and what is not, and the choice of which tool to use is certainly not a purely objective one. Hence, choosing the right tool for the analysis can help rationalize and legitimize certain strategic actions aligned with the objectives the decision maker already had before using the tool, and those objectives could be explicit or implicit. Of course, the reasons for using a particular tool might also be driven by a desire to find or create something new rather than confirm what was already intuited. However, the pre-existing ideas that the strategist has about the situation often direct the choice of the tool. If the issue is perceived to be internal to the organization, tools that help to develop the resources to meet the future demands of the organization appear most apposite; if the problem is perceived to centre on finding customers, tools that help identify new markets to enter are likely to be chosen. While this makes sense and is often a smart way to choose the right tool, what if the problem is not where the pre-existing idea suggested it would be? For example, a firm might be tempted to blame disappointing sales figures on the sales competencies of the salesforce, but perhaps the product offering is not what the customers want. Analysing the situation using a tool that focuses on competencies is likely to push the strategist towards an incorrect conclusion. Hence, we emphasize that you must be aware of your reasons for choosing a certain tool and that you should not rely exclusively on one but should try some others too.

Finally, while it should be an obvious caveat, it is worth stating that the use of tools should be restrained. It makes little sense to use a sledgehammer to crack a nut. If the decision appears to be of little consequence, or the investment bears little risk in contrast to the time and effort it takes to use the tools, it is probably better to just use intuition rather than embark upon the time-consuming process of analysing the decision and trialling several strategy tools. Nevertheless, after some practice, the use of some of the rudimentary strategy tools becomes part of the intuitive process of the strategist. The experienced strategist is aware that strategy tools can be used in many ways; they can serve as instrumental problem solvers, information generators, inspirers of social interaction, or constructors of the strategy process (Wright et al., 2013). Strategy tools serve to help managers devise strong strategies and make better decisions, and if they are to extract the maximum benefit from the tools available, strategists should understand the workings of more than one tool, use such tools creatively and often, and be able to select the most appropriate ones to address the key issues they face.

In summary, strategy tools cannot think or implement projects for managers; that is the work of the manager using them. However, they can stimulate thinking, help to provide a better understanding, and from there support making the best possible decisions in the process of crafting strategy.

5 Common Strategy Tools

The most popular tools among practitioners are arguably the simple ones that do not demand excessive effort or special knowledge. The popularity of the tools is primarily based on their simplicity and ease of adaptation, then the fact that clearly designed tools are easy to remember, and finally that well-known tools are used because they have acquired legitimacy among strategists (Spee and Jarzabkowski, 2009). Gunn and Williams (2007) suggest that the use of strength, weaknesses, opportunities, and threats (SWOT) analysis, various benchmarking methods, and critical success factor analysis stand out in terms of their use by the vast majority of commercial organizations in the UK. Other studies on the use of strategic tools have also highlighted scenario-building methods and various analysis of resources, competencies, capabilities, or key success factors. In addition, PESTLE analysis and its variants and the balanced scorecard are ranked highly in many studies. (For studies on the use of strategy tools, see e.g. Clark, 1997; Frost, 2003; Gunn and Williams, 2007; Stonehouse and Pemberton, 2002.) A 2017 literature review study (Berisha Qehaja et al., 2017) of twenty-seven different studies investigating the use of strategy tools suggests that large and small organizations use tools differently, as that use also differs in developed and developing countries. It also confirms our impression that there are considerable differences across studies in terms of what is considered a strategy tool. The inherent weakness in most tool-usage studies lies in their use of predetermined lists presented to survey respondents to choose the tools they use. While this is practical, it is questionable if this approach captures the full spectrum of strategy tools used. It is a questionable point whether the respondents in these surveys understand strategy and strategy tools in the same way and realize that they might be using strategy tools other than those listed among the alternatives.

While this Element does not evaluate the popularity of tools as such, we do introduce some of the best-known, much-used classic approaches in this section. We would expect that anyone calling themselves a strategist would not only have heard of these but have an understanding of them at a general level at least.

SWOT analysis. The SWOT analysis (strengths, weaknesses, opportunities, and threats) was developed as long ago as the 1960s, but it is still one of the most widely used strategy analysis tools and one that has been applied to serve a multitude of purposes. SWOT is well-known and widely used because the idea is beautifully simple and often useful. The idea of SWOT is to build a synthesis of a current situation to support strategic decision-making. Nevertheless, to be truly effective, a SWOT analysis requires a considerable amount of background work and understanding on the part of its implementer. Other types of analysis of the competitive environment and customers (such as PESTLE and the five forces) and those focusing on the capabilities and resources of the firm (e.g. VRIO) may be needed to generate a meaningful SWOT analysis. A proper SWOT cannot be done in a short time frame, despite the claims of some of its most vociferous advocates. SWOT is often criticized for being too simplistic, and it certainly does have issues relating to how different things are categorized into its four quadrants. It is difficult to determine if certain events should be assessed as opportunities or threats to a company; for example, specialized knowledge of a particular technology could be interpreted as a strength of the company, but such specialization could also constitute a weakness in that it blinds the firm to the benefits and opportunities provided by other technologies. However, if these issues are made visible and discussed during the process of using SWOT, the tools can be a very useful starting point from which to launch problem analysis. Another well-known issue with SWOT relates to it not being dynamic. SWOT does not provide direction to strategy. It only gives an insight, a snapshot, of the current situation; but snapshots are nevertheless sometimes quite useful. However, if a strategist fails to diligently study and reflect the real strengths and weaknesses of the firm, or the opportunities arising from and threats posed by the environment, the SWOT process is likely to produce a long list of obvious elements that are of little use to a decision maker. The key is to be highly critical and challenging to arrive at the real strengths or capabilities that definitely confer competitive advantage and to be honest about the organization's shortcomings. Another important aspect, and one that is often forgotten, is to ensure that having identified strengths, weaknesses, opportunities, and threats, the analysis draws sound conclusions and outlines feasible potential courses of action. That involves directing focus towards how to benefit from the current strengths and reinforce them; how to mitigate the effects of the weaknesses or eradicate them altogether; how to ensure that the opportunities identified are exploited; and also how threats might be converted into opportunities or at least how to counter or remove the impact of the identified threats. However, SWOT itself does not provide any means for weighing, ranking, or prioritizing the issues recognized during the analysis (Helms and Nixon, 2010).

Resource analysis: Identifying and analysing core, critical, or key competencies, capabilities, or success factors. The concept of core competences was introduced by Gary Hamel and C. K. Prahalad and describes a set of resources and skills that distinguish a firm from others and hence lay the foundation of its competitive ability. Hence, it is not just what the company is good at but also something that makes a difference to the customers, is difficult for competitors to imitate, and can be applied in multiple markets. Critical or key success factors are terms describing similar issues – the key elements required for an organization to accomplish or exceed its desired goals – but can often be used in relation to products and projects. We suggest that all these concepts aim to describe the system that lays the foundation for the competitive ability of the firm. As a tool for strategy, understanding what makes the firm unique in terms of it being able to deliver value to its customers more effectively than its competitors allows that firm to prioritize investment, actions, and resource deployment. However, scholars do not seem to agree upon the interchangeability or differences between definitions of core, critical, and key competencies, capabilities, and success factors. Hence, to ensure strategists and decision makers are speaking the same language, the process of identifying key capabilities should start with an introduction to and definition of terms. We find a four-layer capability architecture particularly useful for that task (see Vesalainen and Hakala, 2014) but more and less nuanced alternatives do exist. We believe the terms 'assets' or 'resources' describe the tangible or intangible, firm-specific, and firm-addressable basic elements, which are not usually sources of competitive advantage as such. Capabilities, at the second level of our capability architecture, are combinations of resources that are coordinated by activities. They might also be called competencies, organizational routines, or transformation processes. For example, a company might have a set of production facilities and machines (these are assets or resources) that are coordinated by the application of lean production principles and appropriate people management (activity) jointly forming a *capability* that could be called efficient production. These functional capabilities may or may not be core to the success of the company and, on the third level, there would be a layer of *organizational capabilities*, comprising bundles formed of important capabilities. Again, these higher-level bundles need to be coordinated, for example through the use of strategic or business processes forming the organizational-level capability. Fourth, there is the concept of dynamic capabilities, being those activities embedded in the coordination processes that either leverage the coordinated, planned deployment of resources or develop other capabilities through learning and/or the improvement of an existing capability or resource base.

Once the terms and concepts have been agreed upon, the actual identification of all capabilities, competences, or factors may begin. The result is likely to be a rather long list, and identifying which items qualify to be called key, core, or critical will require some critical screening. That screening process might, for example, employ the VRIO criteria and might be accelerated by asking whether there is solid evidence that the identified factors are real, meaningful, and create value. Ultimately, the process is subjective and only applicable to implementing decisions on the basis of recognized critical success factors, core competencies, or key capabilities. Hence, for something to happen, it is important that the people involved first agree on what are the firm's key, core, or critical competencies and then ascertain its capabilities and the issues it faces.

Probably the best-known resource analysis tool, *VRIO*, started with the famous VRIN framework devised by Jay Barney (1991). Barney was interested in a how a firm could utilize its resources to deliver sustained competitive advantage and concluded that a firm's resources should ideally be *valuable*, *rare*, *imperfectly imitable*, and *non-substitutable* – the set of qualities that gave rise to the acronym. Those criteria suggest that only resources that bring value can be a source of competitive advantage and resources that are widely available or easily imitated, or easily substituted by other resources, will rarely do so. Barney (1995) developed the VRIN analysis to incorporate the organizational ability to exploit resources, in what became known as the VRIO analysis. The new model, also stemming from resource-based theory, suggests that firms review their resources to discern if they are *valuable*, *rare*, *costly to imitate*, and *organized* in such a way that the firm can capture their value. Resources are valuable if they can be employed to reduce costs or increase revenue. They are rare if competing firms do not generally possess the same resource. Imitability often relates to resources that are complex and intertwined with the value creation processes of the firm. For example, a Nobel Prize–winning scientist might be recruited by the competing organization, but an entire research team with a culture of excellence is far more difficult to copy, acquire, or substitute with another. Machines, manufacturing facilities, or good retail locations can usually be easily acquired by competitors, whereas image, brand reputation, or long-standing supply partnerships may be far more time-consuming and difficult to copy. Everything can be copied, but the question is how long it takes to do so and how much money is required. The question of organization is about the ability to make the best use of the resources. Even the most valuable, rare, and inimitable of resources might be useless if an organization cannot create an organizational environment that fosters value creation.

Benchmarking. Rather than being a single branded tool, benchmarking is more of an approach with many potential applications. The idea of benchmarking is to learn from the best practices of comparable firms or sectors and transfer that learning into the context of the benchmarking organization. The idea is not to copy directly but for a firm to compare its own processes or practices in a particular area against those of the best exponents and then adapt the learning to its own operations. Benchmarking can be *internal*, in that it compares processes, practices, and outcomes across the business units of the firm; alternatively, a firm might employ *competitor benchmarking* that seeks to identify the best-performing organizations in the firm's own industry. However, acquiring detailed knowledge of the working practices of directly competitive organizations can be very challenging, and therefore conducting *functional benchmarking* across industries may be more feasible in many cases. That might involve looking at the best practice in customer service, logistics, or marketing, irrespective of industry. The process of benchmarking starts from strategists thoroughly understanding their own business and evaluating the most important areas for development. Having selected those areas for development, the strategist seeks to establish benchmarks by identifying best practices and learning how the industry-leading firms work in the context of the issues identified as targets for development. It is important that a firm employing benchmarking clearly identifies differences between the benchmarked processes and its own before it sets improvement targets. Having done so, it will probably have to accept that the optimal processes identified by benchmarking will require some degree of adaptation before they can be implemented. A firm seeking to grow by identifying and adopting benchmarks must ensure that it has designated measures, indicators of success, and evaluation processes in place to ensure it is progressing; if it does not, it risks making changes for changes' sake.

Analysing the environment or industries. Among environmental analysis tools, the PESTLE framework (which analyses political, economic, social, technological, legal, and ecological factors), serves to impose some order and understanding on the environmental factors affecting the organization. There are a number of versions of the tool, and an internet search quickly reveals PESTEL, ETPS, PEST, STEP, and STEEPLED variants of the tool. The simple (but effective) idea of PESTLE is to list and consider issues in the organizational environment within its different categories. The environment a firm operates in can be affected by an infinite number of things, but there is little point trying to list everything that happens in the world and treat each factor equally in the subsequent analysis. Instead, it makes sense to identify perhaps the five to twenty most important factors and score them according to their magnitude and the likelihood of their affecting the organization. Thereafter, the trick is to focus on those that significantly affect the organization. A war somewhere in the Middle East is not quite so important for a local pizza franchise as it is for a firm involved in arms manufacturing. However, the local town council planning to build a new road bypassing the village the pizzeria operates in might be a matter of great importance for that particular pizza business but of no consequence for the arms manufacturer. Having selected potentially impactful environmental factors, it is then important for a business to evaluate the relevant timescale in which they could exert an effect and then to ideate some scenarios on *how* those developments might affect the organization. Finally, if a business can identify the truly significant change drivers for the organization (which are often combinations of different factors), it can generate the key insights that will equip it to create an effective strategy. The change drivers identified in a PESTLE analysis are often important inputs for any subsequent SWOT analysis, particularly in terms of external threats and opportunities, and the two tools can be used together to great effect.

Probably the best-known of the industry analysis tools, and also a form of environment analysis, is Porter's five-forces framework (1980/2008). The five-forces model draws from industrial organization economics to assert that the structure of the industry, the number of buyers and sellers, product differentiation, barriers of entry, the relation between fixed and variable costs, and vertical integration are the main determinants of business performance. Porter suggested that a firm should position itself in an industry that is favourable to it and then focus on ensuring the competitive forces remain favourable; and if those forces become unfavourable to the firm, it should move to another business. Hence, the point of the five-forces model is to help the firm to investigate if doing business in a particular industry is attractive or not and to show how a firm can protect its competitive position in its chosen industry. The analysis can be adjusted to focus on the firm's current industry or another in which the competitive forces may be more favourable. The five competitive forces that ought to be analysed are the threat of new entrants; the threat of substitutes; the bargaining power of customers; the bargaining power of suppliers; and intra-industry rivalries. Effective use of the five-forces model does tend to demand a very accurate definition of the industry, and it is probably wise to consider some sort of analysis of the strategic groups before venturing into five-forces territory; for example, the airline industry can be very difficult to analyse as a whole and the effective forces are very different in different sectors of the airline market, but meaningful analysis could be conducted in say the intercontinental air-freight field or for the leisure flights market in Europe. It is also important to note the overlaps and integration between traditionally separate industries as well as the maturity of the industry in question. For example, personal computer, mobile phone, and camera manufacturers today largely operate on the same playing field.

Value chain and systems. The value chain concept, developed by Michael Porter, is used to describe the process through which different resources and raw material inputs are obtained, turned into finished products, and sold to create value for the customers. The value chain analysis aims to identify ways in which each step in the process could be made more efficient, in order to deliver value at the lowest possible cost. Competitive advantage can be created in any of the five primary activities (inbound logistics, operations, outbound logistics, marketing and sales, and service) of the value chain. The four support activities (suggested to include issues such as procurement, technological development, human resource management, and company infrastructure) in turn do not as such provide competitive advantages but increase the efficiency of the primary activities. The value chain tool is helpful as it breaks down complicated operations into smaller, simpler parts that can then be further analysed using other tools. Arguably, several other tools also build on the fundamental idea of value chains; those include the buyer utility map (part of the blue ocean strategy toolkit devised by Kim and Mauborgne, 2005) that outlines a buyer experience cycle with stages that are not dissimilar to those of the value chain idea from the perspective of the customer (involving purchase, delivery, use, supplements, maintenance, and disposal). These stages can then be enhanced by focusing on different utility levers. (The original examples offered were customer productivity, simplicity, convenience, risk, fun and image, and environmental friendliness, but other levers can be justified or those examples combined.)

While it is clear that a single firm rarely manages the whole chain of value creation from raw material to end user, the concept can also incorporate networks of companies, in which each of the firms manages its own value chain, creating an interconnected value system. Today, these are also sometimes referred to as business ecosystems. Similar to value chains, these concepts help to understand the complicated value creation systems and identify the areas of potential improvement in terms of value or cost created. However, they do little in terms of understanding what is possible and realistic and hence are usefully complemented with resource analysis.

Canvassing oceans. The blue ocean strategy (Kim and Mauborgne, 2005) was one of the most widely sold management books of its time. The blue ocean of the title refers to uncontested market spaces and the book offers a set of tools and frameworks to assist firms in creating them and thus move beyond a 'red ocean' scenario characterized by known markets, defined industry boundaries, and cut-throat competition (that figuratively stains the ocean red with blood). Blue ocean thinking can utilize many tools, so, for example, the *value curve* and *strategy canvas* tools of Kim and Mauborgne (1999, 2002) facilitate strategic analysis and evaluation of the firm's strategic profile against the industry and its competitors. The aim is to identify and create entirely new market opportunities in the blue oceans (i.e. among prospective customers), in contrast to exploiting existing markets or customer segments, as contemplated in the five-forces framework of Porter (1985). In markets marked by heavy competition, the boundaries of industries are typically clear-cut, products are comparable, and competitors tend to be equally strong. In cases like these, firms mainly compete on price and the efficiency of their operations. In a blue ocean scenario, competition is low or non-existent, and therefore a company can more easily achieve financial success. A new area that is free of competition does not need to be radically different or built on technological breakthroughs; instead, the aim of a company is to achieve a value innovation that, if successful, both adds value for customers and reduces the company's expenses. This generally requires the application of a new kind of business logic. Reducing costs and creating added value are generally seen as opposites and goals that cannot be achieved simultaneously. Companies employing a blue ocean strategy should, however, be able to combine these two elements in their value innovation. A value innovation comes about as a result of measures that affect both cost structures and added value for customers. Cost savings can be achieved by cutting or completely removing elements from the product offering. Such elements might include replacing a high level of customer service with self-service options, in areas where other companies in the industry are actually competing against each other by delivering personal service. Added value is achieved by bringing something to the industry that was not there before. Added value also leads to added volume, which again further reduces costs. When searching for a new business idea, entrepreneurs are often faced with a problem: something that does not yet exist is hard to find. Looking for new business opportunities is like assembling single tiles of information into a jigsaw that is sufficiently complete to demonstrate the essence of the business idea. The blue ocean strategy therefore offers companies a systematic method for looking for something that does not yet exist. The greatest benefit of this tool is the way it makes the innovation process something concrete and turns that process into more defined tasks that can be undertaken in different industries or even in the public sector.

Other kinds of canvassing tools such as the value proposition canvas, customer journey map, and market opportunity navigator have appeared too. These all seem to share the idea that, with the help of worksheets, various aspects of strategy can be analysed and condensed to fit onto a single sheet of paper. One of the best-known ones, and also very popular within the start-up scene, is the business model canvas introduced by Alexander Osterwalder. The business model breaks down the business model into segments (key partners, key activities, key resources, value propositions, customer relationships, channels, customer segments, cost structure, and revenue streams) that help to analyse, recognize, and act on areas that can be improved.

Matrix tools. The BCG matrix developed by the founder of the Boston Consulting Group, Bruce Henderson, can be used to evaluate and contrast the product- or business-unit portfolio of a firm against that of its competitors and markets. It was probably one of the very first tools to look at market positioning. While the BCG matrix is simple, it does cover a number of important themes in strategic management, such as market share, life-cycle stage, and the attractiveness of the sector or industry. The process involves looking at the current product portfolio (or alternatively business units or product categories) and locating them into the matrix. The fundamental idea is that a business should have a balanced portfolio of products in terms of cash flow and investments required. Inserting products or business units therefore helps prioritize activities around them and indicate where to allocate resources. The BCG has spawned different versions, but the original suggested the aspects to consider are market growth rate and the firm's own market share relative to its largest competitor.

Products or product categories for which the firm has a large market share are either *stars* (if the market is also growing fast) or *cash cows* (if the market is not growing significantly). The stars represent areas that may warrant additional investment, whereas cash cows offer an opportunity to harvest the potential but should not attract heavy investment owing to the slow growth of the relevant market. In contrast, product or business areas where the firm's market share is low, but the market growth is rapid, represent *question marks*. Such products or business units could become future stars if the firm could successfully grow its market share. Accordingly, question mark products or businesses may be worth investing in and, if carefully selected, could form the basis for the future growth of the company. Products and business areas where the market is not growing, and the firm's market share is low, are termed *dogs*. These products and businesses should be considered candidates for divestment or sale, in order to free up resources for better businesses.

While the simplified advice to divest, invest, or develop products in certain categories may be historically well founded, we would certainly still recommend treating advice generated by a BCG analysis tool or similar with caution. Many firms would attest to how changes in legislation or breakthrough technologies can suddenly change market growth trajectories or the competitiveness of current products. It is therefore wise for firms to carefully consider market growth rates and market shares in conjunction with other forms of resource, environmental, and scenario analysis.

The GE/McKinsey version of the portfolio matrix considers market attractiveness and competitive power (the strength of the business unit or product) but fundamentally shares the same idea of attempting to understand which businesses the firm should invest in and which are potential candidates for divesting. That GE/McKinsey version is more nuanced than the original; the market attractiveness is not just about growth rate but many other issues could be considered. These could include issues such as industry size and structure (a strategist could use Porter's five forces to do this), trends, changes, and seasonality in prices, demand or supply factors, as well as macro environmental factors (for which the strategist could use PESTLE). The other dimension, consideration of the firm's own competitive strength, includes not only current market share but also market share growth compared to rivals and also consideration of issues such as brand strength, resource base (a VRIO analysis would be useful here) or supply chain strengths, flexibility, or customer loyalty (value chain analysis).

Both portfolio matrices help to prioritize the use of resources and clarify how different business units or products perform. This may help to identify the steps needed to improve the overall profitability of the business portfolio. However, either matrix can only provide a snapshot of the situation and cannot really account for the potential synergies that may exist between the different products or business units. As such, the two differ mainly in their appearance and how comprehensively they analyse the business. It is, however, important to note that more comprehensive is not always the best choice. The McKinsey version may be more sophisticated, in that it takes account of more issues, but it also introduces more room for error as it invites the strategist to assess multiple, often very subjective, and non-measurable issues. The McKinsey version is also the more laborious and costlier to implement and may require input from consultants, whereas the simple market share and market growth numbers required by the basic BCG matrix are often more readily available and can serve as adequate proxies.

A third classic and well-known matrix tool, the Ansoff Matrix, is not to be confused with the above-mentioned variants. The Ansoff Matrix focuses on the product–market strategy. The aim of the classification is to envisage future growth in terms of existing and new markets, as well as existing and new products, and thus create four quadrants of growth opportunities. Market penetration strategies focus on existing products in current markets and existing products that can also be taken into new markets. The existing markets can be further exploited with new products, or new products can also be inserted into entirely new markets, thus creating a diversification strategy.

An idea that is easily combined with and complementary to matrix thinking is that of industry and/or product life cycles. The life cycles depict the various stages in which businesses and products operate. Typically, those stages are reported to be start-up/launch, growth, maturity, and decline. Each stage can last for varying periods that may extend to days, months, or even years depending on the product category or industry.

Balanced scorecard. The balanced scorecard (BSC) developed in the early 1990s is a relative youngster among strategy tools. It has quite quickly become a standard element in the toolbox of any strategy worker. The BSC was originally developed by Robert Kaplan and David Norton to complement existing financial accounting indicators measuring the financial performance of the organization by incorporating more operational, long-term issues such as those affecting personnel or customer satisfaction, and as such the BSC was not originally considered a tool for strategy at all (Kaplan, 2009). However, the BSC established its own position separate from mere management accounting methods because it distils the strategy of the organization down to four essential viewpoints on the business: financial, customers and stakeholders, internal processes, and organizational capacity for learning. The BSC works by directing the attention of management to the causal relationships between and within these elements. For each element, the company sets strategic objectives, identifies critical success factors to achieve them, defines key performance indicators and measures for success, and develops action plans to achieve those measurables. Over the years, the BSC has been extended to include additional tools and processes, so that current versions of it can serve as an overall strategic management system also in public or non-profit organizations. The relatively concrete and measurable approach of the BSC makes it a popular and widely used option in the strategist's toolbox. Despite its merits, the BSC can be criticized for being inward looking and for being primarily useful for optimizing the current operations of the firm. That is a worthy aim in many situations, but in dynamic markets the greatest challenges may relate more to integrating innovations and quickly changing the business logic of the firm rather than optimizing its current operations.

Scenarios. Scenario planning (sometimes also called contingency planning) methods respond to the absence of knowledge in relation to how the business environment will change in the future. The idea is to identify a specific set of uncertainties and attempt to model what might happen if certain parameters of the business change. Scenarios might be described as manuscripts about the future. Contrary to popular belief, scenarios are not so much about making accurate predictions about the future but estimating possible chains of events or plausible development paths. Hence, scenarios deal with two worlds: facts and perceptions. They explore the facts so as to gather and transform information, develop paths to the future, and generate new ideas and perceptions of strategic importance. The various scenario techniques generally include three elements: (1) descriptions of today, (2) descriptions of the different future states, and (3) descriptions of how the two relate to each other. The process involves trying to identify what events or chains of events would have to occur for the current situation to develop into each one of the future alternative scenarios.

Scenarios can be constructed on different levels, relating to the world in general, to the immediate business environment, or to certain sectors. Scenarios might be described, for example, as *plausible, likely, unlikely, favourable, threatening,* or *aspirational,* depending on the assumptions made. Usually, however, several future scenarios are constructed so they can be contrasted. The different types of scenarios could be split into two different categories: *explorative scenarios* investigate past and current trends and continue from there towards the future. By changing parameters relating to such issues such as economic growth, consumer values, political development, or competitor actions, the strategist hopes to find logical and likely paths of development. To contrast with these most likely developments, alternative paths might be developed that encompass less likely events. The strategist might then be asking *what-if*-type questions, such as: What if something unthinkable happens in the presidential elections? What if an international trade war begins? What if consumers really start to vote with their wallets for green solutions?

The other category is the *goal-oriented scenario.* This is based on a vision of the future that envisages what state the company would aspire to be in at a particular point in the future (or the scenario might be based on some other level of analysis). These scenarios are built by working backwards from the future state and strategies created that could support those events happening. The aim is to produce a description of the events that would need to happen for the organization to reach the desired state. One simple exercise that can help with that task involves writing a newspaper article on the company set ten years in the future that details the firm's status and outlines its route to success. A variation of this is a technique called inversion thinking, which is based on the idea of avoiding mistakes that prevent a firm achieving its goals by flipping the goal you actually want to achieve to envisage the opposite outcome. For example, if you have a goal of making money through building a property portfolio, inversion thinking would encourage you to imagine a situation where you lost your money by investing in a property that appeared very cheap but which proved a poor investment. If you can discern reasons for that property not gaining in value – perhaps owing to it being in a poor location, there being little local employment, it having underlying structural issues, and so on – you will devise your own cautionary checklist to apply before purchasing property. In other words, thinking of a situation where everything has gone wrong, and figuring out what might have caused the failure, can offer clues on how to be consistently not stupid.

In terms of strategy, the aim of all scenario-based methods is to answer the question of what we should do to make a favourable scenario more likely, or what we would do if a certain scenario became reality. Importantly, scenario work will not provide answers about what is going to happen, but it might give answers to what we would do if this or that happens. Scenario work can be easily combined with other methods. The first stage, establishing the current state of affairs, could borrow principles and structure from environmental and resource analysis. The future scenarios could be developed by utilizing different wild cards, unthinkable events added to scenarios at random, and involve an evaluation of how they might affect the course of events. Co-creation techniques and workshops lend themselves to both finding alternative future scenarios and testing the feasibility of the envisioned processes that link the current state with the future scenarios.

Close relatives of scenario planning are system dynamics and various simulation methods. However, these terms usually refer to a more measured view as they are generally utilized through mathematical modelling on a limited set of chosen parameters and estimated causal links and feedback loops between them. An everyday example of scenario thinking in action is the current practice by many mortgage lenders that asks customers to think about a situation in which they become temporarily unemployed or one where interest rates rose significantly and then to consider whether they would be able to keep up with their mortgage payments or at least pay the interest on the capital. Similarly, the European Banking Authority's stress tests, which assess the resilience of financial institutions to adverse market developments, are partly based on scenario thinking. Scenario thinking has many benefits because it forces people to think and develop an alternative plan, but equally the approach can be misleading if the assumptions that the scenarios are based on prove false or irrelevant. While this was only a brief introduction to scenario thinking, there is an excellent publication in the Elements series on scenario thinking by MacKay and McKiernan (2018) for those wishing to read more on these methods of strategic foresight.

The most common strategy tools briefly introduced in this section constitute the basic toolbox for a strategist that illustrates the many alternative angles on strategy work. The tools introduced here may be old and well-worn, but they are popular for a reason. First, they are well-known, taught in most business schools, and hence are readily available for managers to apply in everyday situations without demanding much prior preparation. Second, they are relatively easy to use, albeit a proper analysis still usually requires quite a bit of background work or knowledge of the situation. Moreover, with a little imagination, many of them can also be adapted to suit purposes beyond their original aims. It is good to know the assumptions on which they are based and their various uses, even if you ultimately choose to do something else. If this was all old news, great, then the next section will be more interesting for you.

6 Less Well-Known Strategy Tools

Many managers might well just stick with the classic and common tools they know from the business school or MBA textbooks, but, for the more advanced strategist, there is a wide variety of other less well-known tools available. Our relatively straightforward search through the leading strategy and management journals revealed more than eighty different methods, techniques, and ideas labelled strategy tools by their developers, and here we will introduce a selection of those that might be used instead of, or in addition to, the classic variants. While some are just contextualized variants of the tools examined in the previous section, they might inspire different ideas on what is important, on what the strategy should be about, or introduce different methods of working with the strategic issues they identify. Nevertheless, a word of warning is necessary here: the popularity of a tool is usually a valid indicator of its usefulness, and, in the case of these less well-known tools, we have found little hard evidence that they function especially well or indeed that they are objectively truly useful. However, we think that it is valuable for strategists to be aware of a broad variety of tools that could provide inspiration to those searching for different ways to build better strategy. While we provide no guarantee of their practical usefulness, they have all been introduced in reputable academic journals and, as such, have undergone a peer-review process ensuring they have been subject to a form of sanity check. No one could master all of the available strategy tools, and neither would it be possible to explain how to use all of these tools within the confines of this Element; so, we limit our ambitions here to introducing the express purposes of a number of tools we found inspiring or interesting and to providing readers with a citation to the academic article that is the source of information on those tools. In most cases, a search on the Internet using the tool name will also provide near instant access to more information. We hope that this provides sufficient guidance for readers to develop their own applications that fit their specific needs.

Generic strategy analysis tools. There are a number of very generic frameworks and approaches designed to facilitate the strategy formulation process. That process often begins with a review of the current situation and setting some objectives, which will inevitably vary in scope but might encompass project-, function-, business-unit-, or corporate-level objectives. Researchers have given this stage addressing the process and the product of planning, designing, and constructing the strategy several different labels, including analysis and formulation (Kaplan and Norton, 2008a), diagnosis (Rumelt, 2011), and strategy architecture (Vuorinen et al., 2018). The analytical strategy tools are primarily concerned with revealing issues that firms must address when making strategic choices. Those generic strategy tools comprise different analytical techniques for examining (mapping, identifying, or recognizing) something, usually multiple issues of importance, for instance the macro environment of the organization, industry, markets, organizational resources and capabilities, customers, or business relationships. Hence, generic tools can assist in decision-making at the product, business, or corporate level in terms of, for example, resource allocation, product differentiation, or environmental management.

These types of slightly less-known generic strategy tools include the *Strategy Diamond* framework for designing a comprehensive strategy by illustrating various domains of strategic choice (Hambrick and Fredrickson, 2001) and the three-stage method of strategy making (Christensen, 1997), both of which offer managers a way to formulate and elicit commitment to a coherent strategy. Other generic techniques supporting the strategy development process include cognitive mapping (e.g. Eden, 1990) or those forms aiming to trigger innovation with the help of creativity techniques (e.g. Higgins, 1996). Moreover, there is a planning tool for managing risks in the strategy formulation process called *discovery-driven planning* (MacMillan and McGrath, 1995) developed particularly to assist managers of new ventures when entering unknown territory (e.g. new alliances, markets, or product segments). Some of these generic tools may also assist in executing a strategy, as they can additionally be used as methods of implementation planning. For international firms, the *CAGE distance frame-work* offers an alternative type of environmental analysis. Instead of just identifying the environmental factors, it can be used to explore the various types of *cultural, administrative, geographic*, and *economic* distance appertaining to potential markets (Ghemawat, 2001). While it is argued that globalization and information technology have brought different countries and cultures closer together, the world is still not a homogeneous place where customers and business practices are directly transferrable across national borders. Hence, the CAGE distance framework is suitable for assessing country-market portfolios and opportunities for expansion. The cultural, administrative, geographic, and economic distance of the target markets from those the organization knows well makes different markets more or less attractive and easier or more challenging to conquer. CAGE analysis can be conducted on different levels, for a certain industry, firm, or product. Some other tools analyse the overall situation without specific emphasis on the role of resources, relationships, or the business environment. These include the *strategic position and action evaluation* (SPACE) *matrix* (Rudder and Louw, 1998) used to analyse the competitive position of the organization in terms of both external and internal dimensions. Additionally, the *multi-perspective and dynamic competitive strategy* model (Shay and Rothaermel, 1999) integrates some existing analytical methods into one framework to illustrate the competitive environment from multiple perspectives.

   Tools focusing on the environment. A great deal of strategy theory and prior research has viewed strategic analysis as a process of the collection and assimilation of data on a firm's strategic position and sources of competitive advantage that are external to the organization. Therefore, a considerable number of strategy tools also have a particularly *external focus* because they analyse the business environment, industry, and competitors of the company in order to establish its strategic position. These types of tools offer a wide range of different measurement methods, frameworks, process descriptions, and classification metrics. The suggested outcomes and the focus of the techniques vary. Some tools target increasing the level of innovation, others recognize new market opportunities or more generic concepts such as competitive advantage, sources of performance, or understanding the industry value chain. There is an array of strategy tools available to analyse the broad macro environment of the organization, including the PESTLE analysis and Porter's five-forces method introduced in the previous section. However, since the advent of the five forces and PESTLE, the array of strategy tools has expanded owing to new tools offering alternative or complementary viewpoints. The *IA³-framework* was designed to map a company's specific non-market environment (Bach and

Allen, 2010). While it is customary to analyse the company environment in terms of competition, customers, and suppliers (as with the five-forces method), Bach and Allen (2010) suggest that companies should also take into account non-market forces and develop a strategy for dealing with governments and other regulators, activists, NGOs, the media, and citizens in general. While these actors may not be directly affecting the business, they shape the environment in which the firm operates. Hence, it may be important to at least identify those parties and their interests, assets, the information they hold, and arenas of influence.

A second group of external analysis tools can be identified that target organizations moving from a macro environment to a more detailed level of external analysis. These tools offer various techniques for analysing the customers and competitors connected to an industry to promote successful competitive positioning. Such strategy tools mainly help their users understand the industry dynamics, assess the performance of competitors, and investigate new market spaces. The external analysis tools in this group were developed to help managers perform functions such as mapping the profit-generating activities in the industry (Gadiesh and Gilbert, 1998) and to identify potential threats from organizations operating on the periphery of the current industry beyond the currently known set of competitors (Brown, 2004). There are also strategy tools for exploring a range of different *what-if* future scenarios to determine strategy under conditions of uncertainty, such as general guidelines for *scenario building* (Schoemaker, 1993, 1995) and a scenario tool for small businesses (Foster, 1993). Some tools combine scenario planning with risk management methods (Miller and Waller, 2003; Slywotzky and Drzik, 2005) or other analytical techniques (Mills and Weinstein, 1996) to improve decision-making and thus financial performance or to reduce or avoid economic losses.

Tools focusing on internal aspects such as resources. Management often searches for a basis for effective strategy among the resources, competencies, and capabilities located within the organization, and hence many tools for strategic analysis have a clear *internal focus*. They serve specifically to investigate the strategic capabilities of the organization in terms of its resources and competences. The tools in this category offer different forms of resource analysis to investigate the internal capabilities and performance of the firm. Most of these tools incorporate the resource-based view of strategy, which explains an organization's competitive advantage and superior performance by highlighting the distinctiveness of its capabilities. One of the key outcomes managers expect from using strategy tools is to be able to identify and understand the success factors applicable to their firm. The resource analysis tools tend to assume that internal features of the organization and the formulation of a strategic plan based on internal capabilities provide a basis for driving competitive advantage and performance.

Some resource analysis tools focus on recognizing internal strengths and weaknesses (Duncan et al., 1998) or identifying intangible resources that can lead to competitive advantage (Hall, 1993) in a similar way to a SWOT or VRIO analysis. Some others specifically target revealing the value of specific issues, such as corporate culture (Heracleous and Langham, 1996) or socially responsible business practices (McWilliams and Siegel, 2011). The purpose of all of such tools is to improve the understanding of competitively relevant strategic resources and ultimately to help the company establish sustainable competitive advantage. Some of the tools with an internal focus help to assess if current organizational resources, capabilities, and processes suit the chosen strategy or changes made to it. Examples assisting strategy formulation by evaluating the feasibility of the strategy may relate to the capabilities needed to reconfigure the business model (Achtenhagen et al., 2013) or the strategic readiness of intangible assets (Kaplan and Norton, 2004). Building on the idea that strategic flexibility and an ability to reconfigure relevant value chains are key to a successful strategy, Maitland and Sammartino (2012) presented a decision tool that helps to build profiles of an organization's assets in terms of their flexibility. They suggest that organizational assets are deployable to varying degrees, and this flexibility of resources depends on not only whether the asset can be used for multiple purposes (known as its use-specificity) but also if it is valuable to other firms (or its firm-specificity) and if the asset can be easily moved to other locations (or its location-specificity) where it might exert more influence on value creation.

Tools focusing on relationships. There are relatively few strategy tools that focus on analysing the relationships between an organization and its stakeholders. Resource-based theory holds that relationships can also be seen as a form of resource, and hence some of the resource analysis tools may be adapted for relationship analysis. Some of the strategy tools we perceive as relationship tools concentrate on business-to-business (B2B) relationships, while others focus on the relationship between the products or brands of the company and its customers; the latter group would include tools related to consumer analysis and brand management. Analytical tools with an emphasis on B2B relationships incorporate techniques such as the *parenting framework* to clarify the relationship between a multi-business parent organization and its business units (Campbell et al., 1995) and the method for building loyalty in B2B markets (Narayandas, 2005). The *cross-cultural map of moral* *philosophies* (Robertson and Crittenden, 2003) could also be classified as an external analysis tool, but it is interesting in the context of relationships because it was specifically developed to help firms understand the socio-economic environment when operating in different cultural contexts and to assist managers to anticipate the ethical consequences of international strategic decisions. Tools designed to aid customer analysis, on the other hand, serve to classify customers in terms of their potential to generate profitability for the firm (Zeithaml et al., 2001). Such strategic tools can be used to examine the relationship between company strategies and the mechanisms that drive consumers' willingness to pay (Priem, 2007). The tools designed to help understand the relationship between the customer and different product attributes, like the attribute, categorization, and evaluation matrix, or *ACE matrix* for short (MacMillan and McGrath, 1996), or between the customer and the brand, like the *brand report card* (Keller, 2000), are also included in this category. Marketing literature is likely to offer further tools for customer and consumer analysis, but, interestingly, customer analysis tools were not captured in our searches for strategy tools despite the key role they have in successful strategies. Most of the tools for relationship analysis are designed to spur sales growth, improve profitability, and trigger greater customer satisfaction and loyalty or deliver a mixture of those outcomes.

Taking strategic action. Strategy is not only about analysis or diagnosis but also about taking strategic action and continuous adaptation. Many of the modern strategy process models suggest that strategy is not only about analysis or about planning but also about taking the decision to implement a strategy or strategies and then ensuring the implementation is effective. Effective implementation is likely to require continuous adaptation, adjustments to changing circumstances, or some sort of corrective action. If analysis is difficult, taking action to implement the strategy as intended is likely to be even harder. The implementation is about action, so it could be argued that no tools can be developed to undertake the necessary strategic actions on behalf of humans. If the strategist is perceived to be like an architect, they will plan buildings with planning tools but if the strategist is considered to be the builder, they might use a hammer, saw, and nails to actually construct a building, and hence, from this viewpoint, a strategist could use strategy tools to implement strategy, not just plan it. While all tools should provide insights into the organization's requirements and indicate potential courses of action, some appear more targeted towards developing appropriate action rather than just analysing the situation. For example, the original balanced scorecard complemented financial analysis with additional perspectives on customers, processes, and learning, while the later strategy map extensions by Kaplan and Norton (2000) linked the BSC approach firmly with the implementation of strategy. Logically, it makes sense to start the implementation by selecting measures, objectives, and initiatives that a preceding analysis indicates are the most promising. *Strategy maps* (Kaplan and Norton, 2000) help to link strategic objectives, critical processes, and operational actions and make the strategy visible in a cohesive and integrated way to all employees across business units. The later extensions of the original BSC (Kaplan and Norton, 2007, 2008a, 2008b) suggest that an entire strategic management system can be built around the BSC. Those interested in the use of strategy maps are recommended to check Irwin (2002), a study that provides an example of how strategy maps can be simplified and adjusted to serve the needs of various types of organizations.

There are of course whole tracts of literature and many books on change management that can be interpreted as tools to guide the implementation of strategies. Probably among the better known is Kotter's (1996) eight-step process for leading change. The process starts by creating an understanding among organizational members that things need to change and by instilling a sense of urgency around undertaking the necessary changes, and the process ends with instituting the change into a new organizational culture. There is a range of other ideas and tools supporting strategy implementation available to managers. Examples include tools such as the Marlow method (Giles, 1991), which suggests a detailed process and mentor approach for increasing ownership in an implementation process, and Neilson et al.'s (2008) strategy execution approach, which emphasizes the importance of clarifying decision rights, designing information flows, aligning motivators, and, only as a last step, making changes to the structure of the firm. Others have suggested change management through *transition management teams* (Duck, 1993), *internal marketing* (Piercy and Morgan, 1991), or *matrix structures* (e.g. Bartlett and Ghoshal, 1990) as general methods for implementing strategies. Various ideas based on the tenets of lean and quality management, such as business process regeneration (Kettinger and Teng, 1998), also offer a more stepwise approach to changing the processes within the firm to implement new strategies.

The majority of tools designed to support implementation have an internal focus offering methods for organizing activities to improve internal processes and the planning of resource requirements and allocations. In other words, they help to identify, develop, allocate, or apply the resources that are required to execute strategic objectives. There are methods for enhancing general process performance (e.g. Kettinger and Teng, 1998; Repenning and Sterman, 2001) or manufacturing performance (Currie and Seddon, 1992) in order to cut costs, safeguard quality, and improve customer satisfaction. The *time-driven activity-based costing toolkit* (Kaplan and Anderson, 2004) helps managers to forecast the required resource capability from future sales numbers. For the growing body of managers who believe that strategy implementation and organizational performance is largely to do with human capital, Bassi and McMurrer (2007) suggest a framework of twenty-three human resource practices relating to leadership, employee engagement, knowledge accessibility, workforce optimization, and learning capacity. It is very likely that a specific stream of human resources management literature offers more tools and techniques for strategic human resource management (HRM), but, unfortunately, no such studies appeared in our search through the literature for tools described as strategic. Nevertheless, there does appear to be a case for considering if the focus of HRM and HRM research should be redesignated as strategic rather than operational as it is currently. Nevertheless, our search of the strategic management journals reveals a current lack of tools designed to support HRM at the strategic level. Despite the many studies conducted on the external environment, we could identify only a couple of tools that expressly state the need to align business operations with the external environment. Those strategy tools involved enhancing process performance by redesigning information systems (Rockart and Hofman, 1992) and developing strategic accounting systems (Brouthers and Roozen, 1999) to match internal processes to the needs and regulations of the current or future business environment. Both of the tools mentioned remain fundamentally about developing internal systems.

Seeking to influence or change the organizational environment in favour of the organization is of course a challenging task, but the patent lack of strategy tools to assist this kind of undertaking is still striking. Issues such as lobbying, managing the business environment, building new product markets to accept innovations that do not yet exist, or creating business ecosystems, while increasingly studied as phenomena, appear to lack the tools and frameworks that could help practitioners master those challenging tasks. For example, the forestry and wood processing industry is facing a global challenge whereby digitization is reducing the demand for printing paper, and the industry is trying to find other uses for its raw material, wood-based cellulose. While there are many new material innovations in the pipeline, such as the exciting prospect of using combinations of wood fibre, wood oils, and/or cellulose to replace various types of plastics, the efforts are being hampered by the absence of some key players who could develop and commercialize these new materials in the appropriate value systems, and hence the market for the new applications of cellulose-based outputs remains elusive. Strategically it would often make sense for large firms to actively create new markets, or as the fashionable expression puts it to build new business ecosystems that utilize their outputs.

Nevertheless, there do not appear to be readily available tools to facilitate such spin-offs or value-system creation projects.

There are, however, some tools originally designed to address the relationship between an organization and other organizations that could potentially be modified to suit the purpose of supporting value-system creation. The existing forms of similar techniques mainly advance business processes and structures related to mergers and acquisition (M&A) actions, strategic alliances, and partnerships, as well as improving the management of social networks and other stakeholder groups. There are methods addressing strategic partnerships such as the *best-fit partner selection matrix* (Cummings and Holmberg, 2012) and the *M&A integration performance framework* (Gates and Very, 2003) and some designed to understand stakeholder relationships and organize activities effectively, such as the *stakeholder management method* (Ackermann and Eden, 2011). However, the tools appear to assume that a strong performance flows from the effective selection of collaborators, but none of them really appear to take a truly relational view focusing on the relationship as such. The assumption seems to be that there is a plentiful market of collaborators that enables companies to simply select good collaboration partners. Sometimes this is indeed the case in established markets, but in circumstances where the innovation is changing the value system and disrupting the existing one, that is less likely to be the case. Establishing strategic collaboration with customers and suppliers requires a lot of effort. The relationship itself between the collaborating firms should be of strategic interest, and such relationships can even form the fundamental strategic logic for businesses (Vesalainen and Hakala, 2014). The relationships with customers and suppliers, especially in B2B markets, may in many situations be the key to, or even the only source of, competitive advantage. Nevertheless, it has proved difficult to locate any strategy tools that would address the need to develop and nurture the network or business ecosystem relationships, let alone assist in creating the organizations and actors in the supply chain that would allow new value systems to emerge based on new inventions that have no market or obvious supply chain, for example.

Re-evaluation of strategy. Several analytical strategy tools identified in the earlier sections of this Element can be used to assess performance, but rarely do the tools specifically target this re-evaluation and adaptation stage. Such methods include cost and profitability reports that help scrutinize financial performance in terms of internal resources (Banker et al., 1996), value-added processes (O'Higgins and Weigel, 1999), or external market factors (Treacy and Sims, 2004). Each can facilitate identification of the sources of strategic success or failure. The *heart of the business* model (O'Higgins and Weigel, 1999) is designed to measure not only the outcome performance but also value-added processes. The SRS (Sources of Revenue Statement) tool (Treacy and Sims 2004) follows the sources of revenue, whether the growth of the company comes from continuous sales to established customers, sales won from the competition, overall market growth, new markets, or new lines of business. The framework developed by Banker et al. (1996) does a similar thing by introducing four accurate ratios for measuring changes in productivity, price recovery, product mix, and capacity utilization.

Sustained business success requires a continuous adaptation of strategy, and practitioners often need to evaluate the performance of the current strategy and then determine if it should be updated. Most strategic analysis tools can also help managers to assess whether their organization would benefit from a new transformational strategy. The repeated use of any analysis tool will generate trends and any measures followed will signal a need to adapt the strategy if it is not delivering the anticipated improvements in performance indicators like revenue, profit, service delivery, or customer satisfaction. When a well-managed organization finds a strategy tool (or tools) that provides metrics or indicators that it finds useful to keep the business on a stable or upward trajectory, it will use that tool regularly rather than as a one-off exercise. However, it is very rare that strategy tools are developed specifically to track the development of strategy or to signal when it is advisable to change it.

To summarize this section, the point of introducing all these strategy tools was not to press you into learning to use them all. There would simply not be sufficient space here to implement that goal. However, if ever we embark on a task not knowing that there are alternative methods available, we risk using the same tools for everything, whether they are the most appropriate to resolve the problem or not. That in turn risks arriving at the same outcomes irrespective of our aim, which is not desirable because we usually implement strategies to achieve something specific. Things that we do not know about are not part of our world and not among the alternatives or opportunities we could choose from. Hence, in the Heideggerian sense, the purpose of introducing these less-known strategy tools and techniques is to make more tools *present-at-hand* for the reader and thus to expand the comprehension of what strategy tools are available. When a situation arises where it is imperative to use strategy tools to achieve something, and when you have a vested interest in what is going on in terms of strategy in your company, you can learn more about them, and soon these tools will become *ready-to-hand*. The ideas presented will transform into something that fits into your individual mesh of actions, purposes, and functions and the ideas presented in a book become real tools with a real purpose. Tools are something you can use to achieve things and, moreover, that you can mix and match as the situation demands; they are not commandments that you must follow slavishly.

7 Using the Strategy Tools

We cannot say exactly where to start, but you should start. People learn not only by reading but also by doing. In our opinion, however, three things can be achieved by using strategy tools. First, as tools provide no definitive answers, they call for an application of judgement on what should be done. Second, instead of choosing from among all possible courses of action, the use of tools reduces the scope of the judgement required and positions problems in the context of the firm. This may help the intuition, and make the subsequent judgement a little more of an educated guess. Third, and perhaps most importantly, the tools provide a common language for those involved in the strategy work to describe and discuss the issues. Yet which tools should one use? Unfortunately, we cannot give you an answer beyond the simple 'Use several'. The choice of the appropriate tool in each situation depends on knowledge you *do not have*. Sometimes you will need to seek out more knowledge and additional viewpoints; sometimes you will need to distil a broad spectrum of information into conclusions encapsulating the essence of different viewpoints. If you do know your firm's strengths and weaknesses well, it makes little sense to spend much time analysing them further and makes far more sense to develop ways to overcome its weaknesses. In other words, once you identify an area of uncertainty, select tools that will shed light on the issues. Study the environment if you do not know how it works or how it reacts to stimuli or investigate which resources are available if you do not know what your organization might be capable of. Use tools that map relationships between things if you are not sure how aspects of the business are interconnected.

A strategy is a dance with uncertainty that stems from the absence of knowledge. Because these knowledge gaps cannot be eliminated entirely, the strategy is always about judgements, and strategy tools can help to arrive at those judgements. However, they do not actually provide the right answers but narrow down the array of issues to the context of each firm or decision. Different tools do this in different ways because the notion of what is important that underlies the tools is different. Hence, the choice of the tools used is an important one, depending on the uncertainty identified. If one perceives no uncertainty, it probably makes no sense to spend time on using strategy tools, just go ahead and make your fully informed, fully rational, decisions. The future will tell how informed you were and how rationally the world around you works. If, however, you are more inclined to believe that there are limits to our understanding of the workings of the world, you will have to identify what you do not know and exercise judgement. Hence, instead of rules on how to choose the right tool to solve your problems, we would like to propose a couple of thoughts on *how* to work with the tools you choose.

Involve your stakeholders in your strategy work. Most firms entrust their strategy work to their top management teams. While it may not be feasible to implement a process that canvasses the opinion of customers, suppliers, and staff at all levels, involving the organization's stakeholders might just prompt some new insights and ideas and help to identify the issues likely to affect the current or a planned course of action. Collective organizational engagement has also been found to mediate the relationship between organizational resources and firm performance (Barrick et al., 2015), so encouraging a somewhat broader involvement in strategy work would appear to make sense. There is of course a counterargument suggesting that innovations do not come from customers but from highly visionary leaders; that argument is best exemplified by the classic quote attributed to Henry Ford stating that, if we asked customers, we would have no automobiles but only faster horses.[4] Nevertheless, it is customers themselves who are often most familiar with the world of the customer. Certainly, while not all customers of all types of businesses are capable of expressing their specific needs and desires, some customers of some businesses do know precisely what they would like to buy. It is apparent that many issues affecting the supply chain could also be addressed with a little help from suppliers following frank and open discussions (Ylimäki, 2014). However, few strategy tools seem to anticipate involving stakeholders, and instead most tend to rely on correct information and insights magically appearing from information systems or data warehouses. Chirico et al. (2011) suggest that participative strategy work functions as an effective coordination mechanism for orchestrating the multiple viewpoints and opinions for performance improvements rather than conflicts. Value co-creation has been widely discussed within the literature on service management and service-dominant logic but does not yet seem to have found practical application in the strategy processes of firms. The idea of involving parties other than top management in strategy work has received relatively little attention in research (Laine and Vaara, 2015). This may be due to the traditional view of strategy as a top

---

[4] According to Vlaskovits (2011), Ford may have been falsely quoted: 'even if Ford didn't verbalize his thoughts on customers' ostensible inability to communicate their unmet needs for innovative products – history indicates that Henry Ford most certainly did think along those lines – and his tone-deafness to customers' needs (explicit or implicit), had a very costly and negative impact on the Ford Motor Company's investors, employees, and customer.'

management activity, and while the top management does participate in this work, the option of involving others has not attracted the attention of scholars specializing in the workings of top management teams.

Link your strategy to the routines in the organization. Strategies can be made for an entire corporation, its business units or functions, and its teams, and can even be applied at the individual level. While strategies targeting the corporation or team require different levels of abstraction and accuracy, any strategy work should link to the daily reality of the organization. Strategy work and the supporting use of tools should not be undertaken in silos that are separated from customers, employees, or suppliers, let alone from other units of the same organization. The use of strategy tools may be helpful here in terms of both feeding information from the bottom up to support higher-level strategies and in turning plans into action. Linking with the previous idea of involving more people in the organization in making its strategy, strategy tools can be used to build a shared understanding of the issues affecting the future of the organization and of the activities that must be undertaken to safeguard that future. What we envisage here is a process (for larger organizations) in which the top management team first drafts a reasonable sketch of the strategy for the entire firm using a limited number (let us say, between two and four) different tools. Heads of the organization's functions should then present their visions for their function and explain the role of the chosen strategy tools to the staff of that function. The tools could then be applied in a series of function workshops with the objective of devising a strategy map for the function. It would be important to conduct the process in key functions in the various divisions of the organization. It might also be advisable to employ an internal or external strategy consultant to ensure that the understanding of the use of tools and the content of strategy is transferred correctly across the different levels. Subsequently, the same process could be repeated in teams within divisions or business units. The use of the same tools across different levels of an organization effectively communicates what is important to the organization and its chosen strategy. Standardized usage of strategy tools also ensures the chosen strategy is linked to reality and to the actions of the people working in the organization. The work conducted at the lower levels of the organization focuses on what the overall strategy means for the unit, and the team at the more practical level feeds information back to the top level on what is actually involved in implementing the strategy and therefore signals necessary adjustments to the firm-level strategy. Such an exhaustive process could not be conducted quickly or without some tensions but would certainly help to build a common understanding of the organization's chosen strategy and facilitate its effective implementation. Simply taking the trouble to educate organizational staff by introducing and using a couple of strategy tools across the different levels of the organization could help it on many levels. Kohtamäki and Einola (2017) report a successful application of this type of thinking in the context of city strategy through the use of the VRIN framework, a value curve, and strategy maps.

Look at your strategy from multiple perspectives. Many firms think of strategy as something that is an application of one method, a perception that is arguably encouraged by commentary on strategy tools rarely indicating how the proposed tool aligns with other available options. However, it is hardly a revelation to suggest that one should look at the issue from multiple angles, not just from one. The balanced scorecard is certainly a good tool, but perhaps it is missing something; maybe strategists should complement this by working on the business model canvas too? Different situations affecting different organizations demand different tools, so it would be wrong to recommend a single method applicable for all. It may be very sensible to involve a broad selection of faculty members in the strategy process of a university, but it may be less useful to ask the opinions of builders about the options for expansion in a construction company. If the organizational leaders believe that strategy is something that is for the top management alone and believes that the process of formulating it should be strictly formulated, it is probably not constructive to attempt to involve organizational personnel in the development of strategy. For some organizations, the strategy process comprises a series of annual meetings that follow a tight schedule and where the outcomes are largely predetermined by the thoughts of the CEO, and such organizations can sometimes seem to succeed *despite* their strategy. In such cases, the strategy process is probably best left to the top management team, because expanding the process beyond that limited group is likely to demotivate staff whose voices are unlikely to be reflected in the eventual outcome. Nevertheless, we dare to suggest that, if starting from scratch and not being bound to involve other people, examining different perspectives using several strategy tools could be a wise course of action. A strategy process that incorporates taking the trouble to investigate and trial multiple tools and viewpoints, diligently analysing the relevant industry, competitors, customers, and resources, and boldly challenging the current business model could well forestall a deterioration in performance before it develops into a full-blown crisis; that said, root and branch reform of an organization's strategy processes is perhaps more easily undertaken when there is a change of CEO. Path dependencies are strong and reversing one's own decisions can be difficult. A new CEO is more likely to be able to devote the appropriate level of attention, time, and resources to investigate, determine, and deploy the tools appropriate to reformulate the organization's strategy.

Switch and mix between the rational and the intuitive. The use of strategy tools can certainly also inject some rationality into strategy work if it is perceived to be too intuitive. Using a strategy tool can then serve to justify people's intuition if the outcomes of using the tool and following the relevant intuition later coalesce. On the other hand, if strategists show signs of becoming overly reliant on the rationality of strategy tools, it might be worth adding some intuitive component to the strategy tools. After all, there are dangers involved in applying rationality to issues of judgement; not only might the tool itself be flawed and ignore some pertinent circumstances but even in the case of precise and full rationality, a purely rational decision may lead the firm into a direction that neither its owners nor stakeholders want. For example, if we conducted an analysis of attractive industries based on purely rational criteria, the most lucrative multibillion-dollar industries might prove to be illicit, such as the counterfeit goods that account for anything up to 7 per cent of the global merchandise trade or human trafficking that is estimated to be worth up to USD 28 billion (Vardi, 2010). Hence, just as gut feelings and intuition vary across cultures, so too do standards of ethics and morality, and that is a fact that should be taken on board when using strategy tools, especially in an international business context.

Consumers as a body are not very rational. They buy things on impulse, often without any cost-benefit analysis or evaluation of opinions matrices and they are affected by many biases. It would be unwise to maintain that buyers in the B2B markets are entirely economically rational either. For example, we might sometimes find it difficult to identify the (economic) rationale for spending hundreds of thousands on a company logo redesign or buying artwork for the walls of the corporate headquarters, yet many corporations have done just that. Arguably, many recent success strategies have resulted from intuition and a marked lack of rational analysis. The iPad was not created through consensus but through intuitive decisions by the Apple management team, and it is hard to believe that any sort of rational analysis would conclude that a single bottle of beer could retail for ninety Australian dollars, as Australian brewer Crown charges for its limited edition Ambassador Reserve. Hence, the role of emotions cannot and should not be underestimated in strategy work. Indeed, this could be the 'black magic' that makes good strategies truly great. Prior studies have found that emotions affect opportunity evaluation and the anticipated regret of missing out has been found to push nascent entrepreneurs towards start-up decisions (Hatak and Snellman, 2017). Even seasoned venture capitalists have admitted following gut feelings to back up their rational analysis of investment decisions (Snellman, 2017). Intuition is markedly different from logical reasoning processes in that it develops from a variety of experiences and is based on initially vague perceptions of the solution to an issue. It is about grasping the issue in outline but also knowing some of the detail and hence pointing in the right direction; and, to us, this is very much reminiscent of how good strategies are constructed in practice. Intuition is widely used, yet it does not require any hard work or brains to say, 'my gut tells me' (Hammond, 2010). We do not know exactly where these intuitions come from and nor do we know how to improve these rationally unjustifiable judgements. However, emotions, feelings, and intuition do not appear as elements in strategy tools. While intuition and feelings can certainly also be wrong, and we would not suggest abandoning the rational logic of strategy tools, what we do suggest is that rational logic can sometimes benefit from being complemented with a dose of fuzziness, which would prompt analysts to be more honest about the 'quasirationality' of strategy work.[5]

Strategy tools can offer extremely efficient ways to reach both correct and incorrect conclusions. We firmly believe that mastering and using several of them, rather than just one, will deliver more correct insights and estimates. We hope that this Element has inspired its readers to become familiar with a broader variety of strategy tools than they are currently confident to use. We also hope we have encouraged readers to discover their own creative ways to use these strategy tools. Knowledge is not static, and strategic knowledge has a life cycle. Knowledge creation, mobilization, diffusion, and commoditization have different implications for each strategist. While strategic tools lend themselves to providing the inputs for many different decisions, we believe there is still room for additional tools that could facilitate more continuous strategic learning. The current pace of change brought about by digitization, robotization, and artificial intelligence makes it important that people try to keep ahead of machines by inventing ever more clever ways to understand the workings of the world, and how our collaborative organizations prosper in it, as well as to create tools to make it better.

Consider whether time and technology will change fundamental assumptions. Technology has made access to information (both correct and incorrect) readily available and is making advances in developing more sophisticated methods (e.g. artificial intelligence or AI) to analyse the available data. The lack of data is certainly not going to be a problem in the future but filtering the correct information and drawing the right conclusions from the data will remain a problem. Even if AI and robots are removing some of the stupidity

---

[5] Hammond (2010) suggests that *quasirationality* resembles rationality in its intent to be a defensible form of cognition, but the process of knowing is not fully logical owing to the absence of sufficient knowledge, the reliance on partially valid information, or a skill in organizing the knowledge.

from the world by making some routine decisions on behalf of humans, the work of the strategist is not going to go away. Instead, the strategist needs to understand the limited rationality not only of people but also of the more rational AI (with its own, inbuilt, programmed flaws, while also accounting for the fact that even as AI attempts to rectify those flaws it will make new mistakes) when making guesses on what is going to happen in the world and how it might react to whatever the company is doing. Even if machine learning and AI helps us to be mostly correct most of the time and cements its place as something that a strategist should account for, we doubt if AI alone will provide us with brilliant strategies. After all, it is often the unusual – and the sometimes extraordinary – that provides the competitive advantage.

Currently, environmental issues are very topical globally, and concern for the environment could certainly change the ways in which companies can exploit natural resources. Hence, we would expect to see strategy tools increasingly taking account of environmental sustainability factors. Some things may become more expensive, perhaps prohibitively so, or the use of certain raw material resources might be banned altogether. On the positive side, emissions trading could also provide some opportunities to earn money. Social media has already changed the ways in which companies and governments can act, and strategists need to take the issues relating not only to their own business but also to the planet and its populations seriously. Such strategy tools should be more dynamic and extend beyond merely influencing a static competitive environment or customer analysis. Strong forces often also create an opposing trend. While the twenty-first century has been all things virtual and artificial, there are already signs that people might be pushing back and starting to embrace the real, live, and simple. Combined with faster communications, even small issues (good or bad) escalate to become big ones at unprecedented speed, making it necessary to have a strong ethical foundation for anything we do. Nevertheless, most currently available strategy tools do not appear to incorporate any ethical or moral dimensions to weigh up alongside the practical, rational, or inspirational ones.

Can market need pay back love? Finally, after applying your best endeavours to choosing and using strategy tools there is a decision to be made, sometimes quickly. We take this opportunity to suggest our own little tool that can be applied to almost any strategic decision-making situation after the basic analysis has been conducted, the chosen strategy tools used, and when you really must make up your mind. We built this meme *Can market need pay back love?* on four questions.

Can we do it? First, there is the very pragmatic issue of being able to implement the decision. Often the resource-based analysis will indicate if we have or can obtain the necessary resources to carry out our strategy. Sometimes this is only a question of doing it, but sometimes it is also about learning it.

Is there a market need? Second is the question of market and customer needs. That is of course not merely a question of necessity but can also encompass needing something for the sake of status, power, differentiation, or comfort.

Does it pay back? Things in business should be worth doing. In its simplest form, this can relate to whether there is money to be made, yet the strategist should also consider other forms of value that implementing the decision will add, be that for the world, for our customers, employees, or other stakeholders.

Do we love this? While it is not all you need, the question of love is an important one to be added to the other more practical ones. Does the strategic decision take us in the direction we want to go or will it make our life miserable? The question of love relates here not only to whether we love it but also to whether the market, our customers, and the rest of the world that is important to us will love what we are doing or, at least, mostly accept it is not the wrong thing to do.

8 Using Strategy Tools Responsibly

Our ability to develop and use tools and technology has made humans the most successful species on this planet. Different tools and technologies are part of our everyday life, and it would be difficult to think how we could survive without them. Strategy tools of course represent the more abstract end of the tools that we have developed, yet arguably they represent the practice of strategy rather than theory of strategy. They are technologies that we use to make sense of and change the world rather than theories that explain the world. Strategy tools are something that we can use to achieve objectives and hence essential help in our aspirations to design better companies, better lives, and better worlds.

Strategy tools help us to find answers on things we do not know, but they can also be used to disguise our opinions as facts. They can be used to search for knowledge for good purposes but also for bad. Depending on the tool, and how the tool is used, they produce different outcomes, depending on the context and social situation in which the tool is being used (Jarzabkowski and Kaplan, 2015). Therefore, users have to take responsibility for the outcomes of using them.

Scientists and companies around the world are currently developing powerful tools such as machine learning and artificial intelligence that will certainly have strategic implications for organizations. While there are already many examples that machines have already become smarter than humans, we should not leave strategy making to computers. Computers have been beating the best of us in the game of chess or poker. Yet the big difference here is that in a game the available options and uncertainties are limited and controllable, whereas in the real world the uncertainty is much greater than in games. The thing we often call 'reality' causes problems for machine algorithms. In particular, human behaviour is something that is extremely difficult to estimate in advance. For example, the biggest challenges for autonomously driving cars are the perception of the environment (Bagloee et al., 2016), interaction, and communication between different agents (e.g. Maurer et al., 2016). Basically, people do unexpected and irrational things in traffic and, arguably even more so, in business. Rationality alone cannot provide a sufficient response to irrational behaviour; we also need to factor in emotion and a tolerance for ambiguity.

Scientist have also taught machines to learn. Logarithms for trial-and-error learning enable a machine to randomly test something new, and, depending on the outcomes, adjust the rules through which it operates. The practical applications are developing fast and will affect, but not remove, the work of the strategist. For example, creativity is often referred to as something that machines cannot learn. However, science is progressing in terms of machine-bound creativity too and, for example, poems have been created using computational creativity (Toivanen et al., 2012). Time will tell how soon and to what extent machine learning and computational creativity will affect the role of humans as creative agents in the strategy process. Even if some real creativity would emerge from artificial intelligence, a development that is not likely to happen any time soon is the ability of machines to understand the *meaning* of whatever is created. What does a certain strategy mean for people, the planet and the life on it?

Understanding human behaviour, creativity, and the meaning of our actions for other people is difficult or even impossible for people too, yet we should not give up trying. Besides strategy tools, we actually have a special skill to do this. We call this empathy and would define it basically as a threefold concept. It is about the ability to see things from others' perspective, the ability to experience what others are experiencing, and the ability to do and enjoy doing unselfish things such as helping others.

Ethical and empathetic considerations are perhaps the greatest challenge for machines but come naturally for most of us if we just let them cloud (in the positive sense) our rationally oriented business judgement.[6] Strategy tools can help us to see other perspectives, maybe even experience them, but they cannot

---

[6] By connecting empathy with ethics we align ourselves with those that think empathy is central to all work in ethics; that without empathy, one will inadvertently harm others.

decide for us what is the ethical course of action. Empathy also fundamentally enables collaboration between agents, collaboration that is necessary because strategies are socially situated. By this, we mean that the effectiveness of strategy depends on the social situation in which it occurs or, put simply, it depends on how other people (and organizations) react to it. Hence, sometimes, even for business organizations, it will be smart to collaborate or even act against the immediate interests of the firm rather than to compete. Strategy does not work – at least not for extended periods of time – unless the stakeholders involved accept it and its consequences. Therefore, strategy tools cannot answer the question of what is the right thing to do, but they can help determine what it might be possible to do.

As Wawarta and Paroutis (2019) suggest, some strategy tools lend themselves to divergent thinking, and others are best suited to convergent thinking. This idea also encapsulates a difference in terms of achieving fruitful collaboration with stakeholders. Tools that produce a number of different potential solutions (divergence) to a problem illuminate the different understandings of what the company should do. A range of understanding might help to introduce and implement strategic changes across the organization. Divergent tools can also be used with customers to generate ideas and to derive wisdom from the crowd. Convergent tools, in turn, help to shape these divergent ideas into a more coherent understanding of what is important (and perhaps critical) for the organization. When strategists and key stakeholders use these tools together, the tools can help with negotiating priorities and, as such, encourage unselfish behaviour, in that the tools might clarify for stakeholders that their own perspective might not be the most important aspect in ensuring the survival and success of the organization. Strategies are created to achieve objectives that management perceives to be important and strategy tools can be a powerful aid in that process. As the clichéd expressions suggest, you get what you measure or you only get what you aim for, so it is important to be very clear on what that aim is. We started the Element by defining strategy tools as *frameworks, techniques, and methods that help individuals and organizations to create their strategies*, and we wish to add these final words: strategy tools are powerful; *use them responsibly.*

References

Achtenhagen, L., Melin, L., & Naldi, L. (2013). Dynamics of business model strategizing, critical capabilities and activities for sustained value creation. *Long Range Planning, 46*(6), 427–42.

Ackermann, F., & Eden, C. (2011). Strategic management of stakeholders: Theory and practice. *Long Range Planning, 44*(3), 179–96.

Bach, D., & Allen, D. B. (2010). What every CEO needs to know about nonmarket strategy. *MIT Sloan Management Review, 51*(3), 41–8.

Bagloee, S. A., Tavana, M., Asadi, M., & Oliver, T. (2016). Autonomous vehicles: Challenges, opportunities, and future implications for transportation policies. *Journal of Modern Transportation, 24*(4), 284–303.

Banker, R. D., Hsi–Hui C., & Majumdar, S. K. (1996). A framework for analyzing changes in strategic performance. *Strategic Management Journal, 17*(9), 693–712.

Bartlett, C. A., & Ghoshal, S. (1990). Matrix management: Not a structure, a frame of mind. *Harvard Business Review, 68*(4), 138–45.

Barney, J. (1991). Firm resources and sustained competitive advantage. *Journal of Management, 17*(1), 99–120.

Barney, J. (1995). Looking inside for competitive advantage. *Academy of Management Perspectives, 9*(4), 49–61.

Barrick, M. R., Thurgood, G. R., Smith, T. A., & Courtright, S. H. (2015). Collective organizational engagement: Linking motivational antecedents, strategic implementation, and firm performance. *Academy of Management Journal, 58*(1), 111–35.

Bassi, L., & McMurrer, D. (2007). Maximizing your return on people. *Harvard Business Review, 85*(3), 115–23.

Berisha Qehaja, A., Kutllovci, E., & Shiroka Pula, J. (2017). Strategic management tools and techniques: A comparative analysis of empirical studies. *Croatian Economic Survey, 19*(1), 67–99.

Brouthers, K. D., & Roozen, F. A. (1999). Is it time to start thinking about strategic accounting? *Long Range Planning, 32*(3), 311–22.

Brown, J. S. (2004). Minding and mining the periphery. *Long Range Planning, 37*(2), 143–51.

Burgelman, R. A., Floyd, S. W., Laamanen, T., Mantere, S., Vaara, E., & Whittington, R. (2018). Strategy processes and practices: Dialogues and intersections. *Strategic Management Journal, 39*(3), 531–58.

Campbell, A., Goold, M., & Alexander, M. (1995). Corporate strategy: The quest for parenting advantage. *Harvard Business Review, 73*(2), 120–32.

Chirico, F., Sirmon, D. G., Sciascia, S., & Mazzola, P. (2011). Resource orchestration in family firms: Investigating how entrepreneurial orientation, generational involvement, and participative strategy affect performance. *Strategic Entrepreneurship Journal, 5*(4), 307–26.

Christensen, C. M. (1997). Making strategy: Learning by doing. *Harvard Business Review, 75*(6), 141–56.

Clark, D. N. (1997). Strategic management tool usage: A comparative study. *Strategic Change, 6*(7), 417–27.

Combs, J. G., Russell Crook, T., & Shook, C. L. (2005). The dimensionality of organizational performance and its implications for strategic management research. In D. J. Ketchen & D. D. Bergh (Eds), *Research Methodology in Strategy and Management* (pp. 259–286). Bingley: Emerald Group Publishing.

Cummings, J. L., & Holmberg, S. R. (2012). Best–fit allianc partners: The use of critical success factors in a comprehensive partner selection process. *Long Range Planning, 45*(2/3), 136–59.

Currie, W. L., & Seddon, J. J. M. (1992). Managing AMT in a just-in-time environment in the UK and Japan. *British Journal of Management, 3*(3), 123–36.

Day, G. S. (2007). Is it real? Can we win? Is it worth doing? *Harvard Business Review, 85*(12),110–20.

Duck, J. D. (1993). Managing change: The art of balancing. *Harvard Business Review, 71*(6), 109–18.

Duncan, W. J., Ginter, P. M., & Swayne L. E. (1998). Competitive advantage and internal organizational assessment. *Academy of Management Executive, 12*(3), 6–16.

Eden, C. (1990). Strategic thinking with computers. *Long Range Planning, 23*(6), 35–43.

Foster, M. J. (1993). Scenario planning for small businesses. *Long Range Planning, 26*(1), 123–9.

Frost, F. A. (2003). The use of strategic tools by small and medium-sized enterprises: An Australasian study. *Strategic Change, 12*(1), 49–62.

Gadiesh, O., & Gilbert, J. L. (1998). How to map your industry's profit pool. *Harvard Business Review, 76*(3), 149–62.

Gates, S., & Very, P. (2003). Measuring performance during M&A integration. *Long Range Planning, 36*(2), 167.

Ghemawat, P. (2001). Distance still matters: The hard reality of global expansion. *Harvard Business Review, 79*(8), 137–47.

Giles, W. D. (1991). Making strategy work. *Long Range Planning, 24*(5), 75–91.

Golsorkhi, D., Rouleau, L., Seidl, D., & Vaara, E. (Eds). (2010). *Cambridge Handbook of Strategy As Practice.* Cambridge: Cambridge University Press.

Gunn, R., & Williams, W. (2007). Strategic tools: An empirical investigation into strategy in practice in the UK. *Strategic Change, 16*(5), 201–16.

Hall, R. (1993). A framework linking intangible resources and capabilities to sustainable competitive advantage. *Strategic Management Journal, 14*(8), 607–18.

Hambrick, D. C., & Fredrickson, J. W. (2001). Are you sure you have a strategy? *Academy of Management Executive, 15*(4), 48–59.

Hammond, K. R. (2010). Intuition, no! ... quasirationality, yes! *Psychological Inquiry, 21*(4), 327–37.

Hatak, I., & Snellman, K. (2017). The influence of anticipated regret on business start-up behaviour. *International Small Business Journal, 35*(3), 349–60.

Helms, M. M., & Nixon, J. (2010). Exploring SWOT analysis – where are we now? A review of academic research from the last decade. *Journal of Strategy and Management, 3*(3), 215–51.

Heracleous, L., & Langham, B. (1996). Strategic change and organizational culture at hay management consultants. *Long Range Planning, 29*(4), 485–94.

Higgins, J. M. (1996). Innovate or evaporate: Creative techniques for strategists. *Long Range Planning, 29*(3), 370–80.

Huff, A. S., Floyd, S. W., & Sherman, H. D. (2009). *Strategic Management: Logic and Action.* New York: John Wiley & Sons.

Irwin, D. (2002). Strategy mapping in the public sector. *Long Range Planning, 35*(6), 637–47.

Jarzabkowski, P. (2005). *Strategy As Practice: An Activity-Based Approach.* London: Sage.

Jarzabkowski, P., & Kaplan, S. (2015). Strategy tools in use: A framework for understanding 'technologies of rationality' in practice. *Strategic Management Journal, 36*(4), 537–58.

Kaplan, R. S. (2009). Conceptual foundations of the balanced scorecard. In C. S. Chapman, A. G. Hopwood, & M. D. Shields (Eds), *Handbook of Management Accounting Research,* Vol. 3 (pp. 1253–69). Amsterdam: Elsevier.

Kaplan, R. S., & Anderson, S. R. (2004). Time-driven activity-based costing. *Harvard Business Review, 82*(11), 131–8.

Kaplan, R. S., & Norton, D. P. (2000). Having trouble with your strategy? Then map it. *Harvard Business Review*, *78*(5), 167–76.

Kaplan, R. S., & Norton, D. P. (2004). Measuring the strategic readiness of intangible assets. *Harvard Business Review*, *82*(2), 52–63.

Kaplan, R. S., & Norton, D. P. (2007). Using the balanced scorecard as a strategic management system. *Harvard Business Review*, *85*(7/8), 150–61.

Kaplan, R. S., & Norton, D. P. (2008a). Mastering the management system. *Harvard Business Review*, *86*(1), 62–77.

Kaplan, R. S., & Norton, D. P. (2008b). *The Execution Premium: Linking Strategy to Operations for Competitive Advantage*. Cambridge, MA: Harvard Business Publishing.

Keller, K. L. (2000). The brand report card. *Harvard Business Review*, *78*(1), 147–57.

Kettinger, W. J., & Teng, J. T. C. (1998). Aligning BPR to strategy: A framework for analysis. *Long Range Planning*, *31*(1), 93–107.

Kim, W. C., & Mauborgne, R. (1999). Creating new market space. *Harvard Business Review*, *77*(1), 83–93.

Kim, W. C., & Mauborgne, R. (2002). Charting your company's future. *Harvard Business Review*, *80*(6), 76.

Kim, W. C., & Mauborgne, R. (2005). *Blue Ocean Strategy: How to Create Uncontested Market Space and Make the Competition Irrelevant*. Cambridge, MA: Harvard Business Publishing.

Kohtamäki, M., & Einola, S. (2017). Participative strategy process in the city of Vaasa. In G. Johnson, R. Whittington, K. Scholes, D. Angwin, & P. Regnér (Eds.), *Exploring Strategy: Text and Cases* (pp. 525–31). Harlow: Pearson.

Kotter, J. P. (1996). *Leadership Change*. Cambridge, MA: Harvard Business Publishing.

Laine, P. M., & Vaara, E. (2015). Participation in strategy work. In D. Golsorkhi, L. Rouleau, D. Seidl, & E. Vaara (Eds), *Cambridge Handbook of Strategy As Practice* (pp. 616–31). Cambridge: Cambridge University Press.

MacKay, R. B., & McKiernan, P. (2018). *Scenario Thinking: A Historical Evolution of Strategic Foresight*. Cambridge: Cambridge University Press.

MacMillan, I. C., & McGrath, R. G. (1995). Discovery-driven planning. *Harvard Business Review*, *73*(4), 44–54.

MacMillan, I. C. & McGrath, R. G. (1996). Discover your products' hidden potential. *Harvard Business Review*, *74*(3), 58–73.

Maitland, E., & Sammartino, A. (2012). Flexible footprints: Reconfiguring MNCs for new value opportunities. *California Management Review*, *54*(2), 92–117.

Maurer, M., Gerdes, J. C., Lenz, B., & Winner, H. (2016). *Autonomous Driving: Technical, Legal and Social Aspects*. Berlin: Springer.

McWilliams, A., & Siegel, D. S. (2011). Creating and capturing value: Strategic corporate social responsibility resource–based theory, and sustainable competitive advantage. *Journal of Management, 37*(5), 1480–95.

Miller, K. D., & Waller, H. G. (2003). Scenarios, real options and integrated risk management. *Long Range Planning, 36*(1), 93–107.

Mills, R. W., & Weinstein, B. (1996). Calculating shareholder value in a turbulent environment. *Long Range Planning, 29*(1), 76–83.

Minzberg, H., Ahlstrand, B., & Lampel, J. (2005). *Strategy Safari: A Guided Tour through the Wilds of Strategic Management*. New York: Simon & Schuster.

Minzberg, H., & Waters, J. A. (1985). Of strategies, deliberate and emergent. *Strategic Management Journal, 6*(3), 257–72.

Narayandas, D. (2005). Building loyalty in business markets. *Harvard Business Review, 83*(9), 131–9.

Neilson, G. L., Martin, K. L., & Powers, E. (2008). The secrets to successful strategy execution. *Harvard Business Review, 86*(6), 60–70.

O'Higgins, E., & Weigel, J. (1999). HOB: A new tool for tracking and increasing value added. *Long Range Planning, 32*(1), 65–74.

Paroutis, S., Franco, L. A., & Papadopoulos, T. (2015). Visual interactions with strategy tools: Producing strategic knowledge in workshops. *British Journal of Management, 26*, S48–S66.

Piercy, N., & Morgan, N. (1991). Internal marketing: The missing half of the marketing programme. *Long Range Planning, 24*(2), 82–93.

Priem, R. L. (2007). A consumer perspective on value creation. *Academy of Management Review, 32*(1), 219–35.

Porter, M. E. (1980/2008). *Competitive Strategy: Techniques for Analyzing Industries and Competitors*. New York: Simon & Schuster.

Porter, M. E. (1985). *Competitive Advantage: Creating and Sustaining Superior Performance*. New York: Free Press.

Repenning, N. P., & Sterman, J. D. (2001). Nobody ever gets credit for fixing problems that never happened: Creating and sustaining process improvement. *California Management Review, 43*(4), 64–88.

Robertson, C. J., & Crittenden, W. F. (2003). Mapping moral philosophies: Strategic implications for multinational firms. *Strategic Management Journal, 24*(4), 385–92.

Rockart, J. F., & Hofman, J. D. (1992). Systems delivery: Evolving new strategies. *Sloan Management Review, 33*(4), 21–31.

Rudder, L., & Louw, L. (1998). The SPACE matrix: A tool for calibrating competition. *Long Range Planning, 31*(4), 549–59.

Rumelt, R. P. (2011). *Good Strategy/Bad Strategy*. New York: Crown Business

Schoemaker, P. J. (1993). Multiple scenario development: Its conceptual and behavioral foundation. *Strategic Management Journal, 14*(3), 193–213.

Schoemaker, P. J. H. (1995). Scenario planning: A tool for strategic thinking. *Sloan Management Review, 36*(2), 25–40.

Shay, J. P., & Rothaermel, F. (1999). Dynamic competitive strategy: Towards a multi–perspective conceptual framework. *Long Range Planning, 32*(6), 559–72.

Slywotzky, A. J., & Drzik, J. (2005). Countering the biggest risk of all. *Harvard Business Review, 83*(4), 78–88.

Snellman, K. (2017). The role of emotions in new venture creation. Doctoral dissertation, Aalto University.

Spee, A. P., & Jarzabkowski, P. (2009). Strategy tools as boundary. *Strategic Organization, 7*(2), 223–32.

Spender, J. C. (2014). *Business Strategy: Managing Uncertainty, Opportunity, and Enterprise*. Oxford: Oxford University Press.

Stonehouse, G., & Pemberton, J. (2002). Strategic planning in SMEs: Some empirical findings. *Management Decision, 40*(9), 853–61.

Toivanen, J., Toivonen, H., Valitutti, A., & Gross, O. (2012). Corpus-based generation of content and form in poetry. In M. L. Maher, K. Hammond, A. Pease, R. Pérez y Pérez, D. Ventura, & G. Wiggins (Eds), *Proceedings of the Third International Conference on Computational Creativity* (pp. 175–9). Dublin: University College Dublin.

Treacy, M., & Sims, J. (2004). Take command of your growth. *Harvard Business Review, 82*(4),127–33.

Vardi, N. (2010). The world's biggest illicit industries. *Forbes Magazine*, 11 June. www.forbes.com/2010/06/04/biggest-illegal-businesses-business-crime.html#1b7493d65b98

Vesalainen, J., & Hakala, H. (2014). Strategic capability architecture: The role of network capability. *Industrial Marketing Management, 43*(6), 938–50.

Vlaskovits, P. (2011). Henry Ford, innovation, and that 'faster horse' quote. *Harvard Business Review, 29*(08). https://hbr.org/2011/08/henry-ford-never-said-the-fast#comment-section

Vuorinen, T., Hakala, H., Kohtamäki, M., & Uusitalo, K. (2018). Mapping the landscape of strategy tools: A review on strategy tools published in leading journals within the past 25 years. *Long Range Planning, 51*(4), 586–605.

Wawarta, C. A., & Paroutis, S. (2019). Strategy tools in open strategizing: Blessing or curse for making strategy more actionable? In *Academy of*

Management Proceedings (p. 16778). Briarcliff Manor, NY: Academy of Management. https://journals.aom.org/doi/pdf/10.5465/AMBPP.2019.270

Whittington, R. (2006). Completing the practice turn in strategy research. *Organization Studies, 27*(5), 613–34.

Wright, R. P., Paroutis, S. E., & Blettner, D. P. (2013). How useful are the strategic tools we teach in business schools?. *Journal of Management Studies, 50*(1), 92–125.

Ylimäki, J. (2014). A dynamic model of supplier–customer product development collaboration strategies. *Industrial Marketing Management, 43*(6), 996–1004.

Zeithaml, V. A., Rust, R. T., & Lemon, K. N. (2001). The customer pyramid: Creating and serving profitable customers. *California Management Review, 43*(4), 118–42.

Cambridge Elements ☰

Business Strategy

J.-C. Spender
Rutgers Business School
J.-C. Spender is a visiting scholar at Rutgers Business School and a research Professor, Kozminski University. He has been active in the business strategy field since 1971 and is the author or co-author of 7 books and numerous papers. His principal academic interest is in knowledge-based theories of the private sector firm, and managing them.

About the Series
Business strategy's reach is vast, and important too since wherever there is business activity there is strategizing. As a field, strategy has a long history from medieval and colonial times to today's developed and developing economies. This series offers a place for interesting and illuminating research including industry and corporate studies, strategizing in service industries, the arts, the public sector, and the new forms of Internet-based commerce. It also covers today's expanding gamut of analytic techniques.

Business Strategy

Printed in Great Britain
by Amazon

80148109R00037